WRITING DEATH.

JEREMY FERNANDO,

# Writing Death.

FOREWORD BY

AVITAL RONELL.

⁞

this work is licensed under the creative commons
attribution-noncommercial-noderivs 3.0 unported license.
http://creativecommons.org/licenses/by-nc-nd/3.0/

printed by lightning source, milton keynes
in an endless edition (version 110606)
ISBN 978-90-817091-0-1

design by MICHELLE ANDREA WAN

uitgeverij, den haag
shtëpia botuese, tiranë
publishing house, new york
出版社, singapore

www.uitgeverij.cc

## CONTENTS

—

9
The Tactlessness of an Unending Fadeout
–AVITAL RONELL

—

29
distress call

—

35
how do i mourn thee?

—

43
stories ... names

—

65
hold, cut, kill

—

75
get over it

—

85
on tears

—

101
adieu

> I don't want to talk about it, for fear of making literature
> out of it—or without being sure of not doing so—although
> as a matter of fact literature originates within these truths.
>
> ROLAND BARTHES, 'A Cruel Country'

For MAURICE JAMES BEINS;

who told me stories …

Words like violence
Break the silence
Come crashing in
Into my little world
Painful to me
Pierce right through me
Can't you understand
Oh my little girl

All I ever wanted
All I ever needed
Is here in my arms
Words are very unnecessary
They can only do harm

Vows are spoken
To be broken
Feelings are intense
Words are trivial
Pleasures remain
So does the pain
Words are meaningless
And forgettable

All I ever wanted
All I ever needed
Is here in my arms
Words are very unnecessary
They can only do harm
—

MARTIN GORE & DAVE GAHAN, *Enjoy the silence*

# The
## Tactlessness
## of an
### Unending

Fadeout … [1]

—

AVITAL RONELL

... murmur, murmur, murmurmur, hmm, capable only of a first reflex, I tell myself. It doesn't need to be a full-blown reflection, she's only asking for a sign, maybe a note. I don't even have to carry a melody. Philippe, Philippe. I can't think straight, oh yes, "Echo of the Subject," the stuff about the caesura, poetry, and muteness. The anthropological hinge in Heidegger: I could do that, maybe. Get in on the subtle takedown, firm yet cautious. I don't know. Too much focus, I can hardly see straight. I need to find a libido pulley. What about the "retreat of the political" or, better yet, the blurb he did for me, yes make it about me, that will stoke the writing engine, not bad, oh come off it, have you lost your senses Superego pounces on me, with the usual "eyes on the prize" corrective, go in the direction of honoring, keep yourself on the sidelines of the commemorative agony, refuse manic compensation, bow the head but go on, as if we could go on, must go on, a "must go on" that warps rapidly into a sneering, "go on, oh just go on," as if I had stretched myself beyond credibility. Already, so soon. Wait, I could render homage to Philippe's hyperbologic, but that's still kind of about me, too much feed for the autobiographical trace, I'm always on the outskirts of the hyperbologic, even when I'm off duty, just hanging out, keeping basically to myself and out of nowhere they say that I exaggerate or invent (Cixous: "When I said that you invent, I did not call you a liar, Avital, you have misunderstood me, *chérie*"). Still too much about me, makes me cringe, I've got to take myself out of the running here, off the table, or whatever they say for self-effacement in mourning. Find a calmer tonality, the missing musical note. Or just drop it. Can't do that. "Is life worth living?" Remember, suddenly in Max Weber. But that has nothing to do with Philippe. Except for the structure of the haunting melody that he depicts. In my head: "Is life worth living?" philosophy's urgent question. Note, *Not*: distress, in German, heavily accented in his work. Maybe I should do something with his reading of "*Dichtermut*" (The Poet's Courage) and the rhetoric of exaggeration; that'll teach them. But now, this is commemorative, remember, I should stay within the precincts

---

[1] A version of this text is previously published as "L'indélicatesse d'un interminable fondu au noir" in Avital Ronell. *Lignes de front*. trans. Daniel Loayza. (Editions Stock, L'autre pensée: Paris), 2010.

of "*Andenken*" (Remembrance), maybe, sticking with the Hölderlin poem to which Philippe devoted so much reflective energy; he went so far as to translate it even and gave the voice over on the film we watched. His voice. Voice over. Over, *über, vorüber,* over. All this on fast spin cycle. Can't do it, no can do, will she be mad at me? After all those pages pledged to mourning pathology and manic economies of writing. Is it OK to say nothing and let him drift away on his own?

On the other hand, can I avoid the narcissism of annexation, of putting teethmarks of ownership on him, taking a bite out of him, as Derrida evokes with his run of morsels, the sounds that go with remorse, *mort,* the whole gamut of bite-size instances of incorporation. I could do it nicely, with a toothy grin, make him mine, open wide and introject. "He's a part of me, Philippe, *my* Philippe, I love him like a ... Here are some story lines to prove it." No, kind of inevitable, swallowing him whole at this time, but can't do that either, too unconscious, too indecent, part of the facile "appropriation" of the missing companion. What about *dépropriation,* I can do something about his tendency toward disinstallation and this way climb into the think tank of his oeuvre. He taught me that Nietzsche was the absence of an oeuvre, everything being organized around the hole punched into an unclosing work. He read Heidegger to us, made Heidegger bearable, as Susan says, he provided us with the e-z pass to Heidegger, though never making it easy, actually making it all that much harder, taking off the blinkers, calling up the solar storm of an unbypassable thought. Can't do this. It's too soon. Too dark. I can sway instead to phantom music, but am incapacitated as concerns the rest of the grammar of summation. Something like a dialectical summation would be called for now, absurdly difficult, requires some lucidity and a measure of distance. My swaying and staggering hasn't reached the Nietzschean *Dis-tanz.* I'm a scholar, I should be able to produce, "poiesize," something blindfolded at this point, on the verge of consciousness, at this point, I say to myself. How can I numb myself on automatic and ticker type out my sorrow? Maybe I can draw up lists, checking off the themes and topoi, the lexical innovations that he created and the vocabulary of being that his work calls up.

That would be a contribution, I say to myself, just start a ledger, become a bookkeeper of the departed friend. That's a service in itself, I don't need even to put a "self" in there or sing along to the bouncing ball of mourning and mania, just start transcribing, straightening columns of his entries into the world of thought. I see only advantages to such a procedure, topped off by an affective bonus: I can stay numbed out this way, at most switching here and there into DJ mode, putting some work into relation with itself, scratching and popping but not getting involved or pumping up energy that I don't have for thinking or bringing things together. It's too soon. I am depleted, washed out by Philippe's *disparition*, as they say. Here's what I can do for you. I'll accept the job of zombie transcriber, as secretary of the phantom (which is all I ever wanted to be anyway), I'll just be writing shorthand, taking it down without any blown up myths of interiority or authorial inspiration or subjectivizing winds for my sails. This way "I," barely a punctuation mark, could ride into a crease in his thinking of the "*défaillance* of myth," I'll come in from another side of the faltering subject. Maybe I can offer a survey of what Denis has brought to light: what it is that we underline when we read someone, he asked in the memorial. That's what I can do, I'll accumulate all the underlinings and maybe collect those of the other mourners. What have they underlined in his work? What kind of an appropriative line does the underscore bring up to us at this time? Philippe would approve this move, I believe. He'd understand my distress and the reversion to a line. Maybe I'll stay close to Philippe's distress, make it my home, I say to myself. I can tally and tabulate, start up the books, press "distress."

It could be that no one among the great French philosophers has understood distress as well as Philippe Lacoue-Labarthe. He rode the wave of Hölderlin's phrase, "*in dürft'ger Zeit*" (in hollowed time) and found his way through Heidegger's *Not* until the end of an impressive oeuvre. Lacoue-Labarthe blended tropes of distress into an unparalleled rhetoric of ethicity, without turning this into a burden or inflating the accepted currencies of prescriptive discourse. He often stood alone, even though he was the most outreaching of thinkers who partnered up momentously with Jean-Luc Nancy, Jean-Christophe Bailly and a number of others. His political thought extended to institutions as it retreated from their deluded complacency and schizoid evacuations. He never gave up on poetry, never; he was among the only rigorous philosophers, apart from Schopenhauer, sometimes Nietzsche and maybe also Adorno, to have heard music and let it in, asking it to speak. He had perfect pitch for historical disaster and the caesura. He cleared terrible abysses and scanned the losses that pockmark something like a rhetorical unconscious. He stood up together with Nancy to read Lacan for Lacan—Lacan characteristically blasted his own disciples for not being able to match the acuity of *Le titre de la lettre*, where they exemplarily took on the master psychoanalyst. His care and carefulness remain unprecedented ...

*\*\*\*\*\*\*\*\*\*\**

I'll pull in my oars, sit with the stillness. Ok. Well, not ok, but it's the best I can do under the circumstances. I am so under the circumstances, so distressed, blue: "Blue" was one of Philippe's last words according to Claire Nancy. "What do you mean you don't feel well? Are you talking mentally or physically?" "In a bluesy kind of way," he had said in the hospital, shortly before the end. His attachment to the blues, in the musical mode, I mean, is by now legendary. One could say, stretching things, that it provides the upbeat for the Wagner readings, returning in a contrapuntal sort of way to transpose, if only on a track set on mute (as Freud says of the death drive), the musical ideologies and pernicious identitarian backdrop of national aestheticism. "The Blues contra Wagner": Nietzsche could have pulled this off, with his sense of ensemble and fracture. The blues separate off from the heavy Germanic purposefulness of destinal meaning and the abyssal euphoria of Wagner. It is as if, for Lacoue-Labarthe, Nietzsche's criticism of Wagner (which Heidegger, for once, seconds and upholds) could bypass the Bizet aberration paraded by Nietzsche in his early contra-Wagner phases and feed directly into the blues. Philippe Lacoue-Labarthe was seized by the blues at the limit of finitude, when taking his last breaths.

In my years of fond and often intense friendship—the kind that implies reliance, intimacy and the infinite conversation, as well as a sense of the irony of the whole thing—Philippe would often self-gather, I thought, in the inenarrable vicinity of the blues. It shows up again, the attachment to the blues but for the most part as "jazz," in *Le chant des muses*, the "*petite conférence*" that Lacoue-Labarthe offered at Le Centre dramatique national de Montreuil in conversation with a group of children meant to show "*un mouvement d'amitié traversant les generations*," according to the preface of the book given to me by Micaela Kramer, who had been present at the event. The model for this sort of encounter and address was Walter Benjamin's radio program between 1929 and 1932, meant for children. Philippe chose to speak to the assembled children about music and philosophy, about the muses and the blues, the Greeks and *rhythmos*—even about music as "*une production (une poïesis 'technique'): un art.*" I am drawn now to this scene not only because Micaela, beloved student, brought it to my attention as I was casting about in despair of his loss, dispirited and speechless … I thought I'd just listen to music, that's what I'll do, I'll listen to music with and through Philippe, stereophonically hooking him up to Nietzsche, who put the spirit in music despite all the disclaimers, I'll just sit and listen to his music, Micaela gave me the idea and the Jungian analyst with whom I had taken a course at the ashram said to dance to the departed, to sway with what still clung of this spirit of music. Maybe I'll ditch the ledgers I've been preparing and just tune his thought to the music that flourished through him. Maybe Nietzsche wasn't off range when clipping spirit to music, trolling after tragedy. That would be one "reason" to switch on the music channel when conferring with or even about Philippe. Anyway, in his magisterial work, *Musica Ficta*, Philippe himself says that the question of music is never a question of music alone.

The other reason to go the way of *Le chant des muses* now (even though in one of his articles Jean-Christophe Bailly wonders if we can even say "chant" any longer or revive the spirit of poetry in terms of song or *Gesang*)—the other "reason" was that Philippe in this work often and by means of subtle protocols precedes the age of reason—precedes himself, in a way, since he was the most reasonable of Daseins I have known and his elaborations were always, if one can say this, severely reasoned. This other reason which, paradoxically, renders him even more reasonable, was that I felt he could communicate with my age, which to date has not achieved the age of reason, but crawls at sometimes childish levels of incomprehension, gasping for the breath of understanding. My need for starting over, my resetting compulsion, are colossal, the only large-scale quality that I can display about myself. So he crouches to my level, gets small without talking down. He addresses children, teaching philosophy, introducing music. Teaching children, he addresses me, I say to myself, instigating a minority report, allowing my regressions and confusions, my still orthodox philosophical experience of astonishment. He licenses the children's menu of *thaumazein*, enlisting a vocabulary of original bewilderment (my German colleagues prostrate themselves before this word, adoring it unambivalently, for once), basing his carefully worded assertions on what in another context I trace to the weighted conjunction of *stupor* as it crosses over into *stupidity*. Clearly another story and altogether inappropriate for a commemorative text, the matter of stupidity, even though it's point blank on the side of the death drive. Also, it reminds me how Philippe would not hesitate to say things like, "I have no idea what he's getting at," when for instance I queried him on a philosopheme in Deleuze, or when he claimed confusion over Levinas's "otherwise"-directed apportionment of being.[2] But that was on the side of knowledge, so "confusion" would be going too far: Philippe saw no reason for reserving an "otherwise" zone for being: "*mais c'est l'être*," he said to me insisting on the expansive range of being,

---

[2] Here's the story as it was told to me: Philippe had claimed semi-publicly in Strasbourg that he couldn't understand what Levinas was getting at with "otherwise than Being," and he voiced his consternation quite vociferously in a semi-public discussion at the university. In the next days Levinas himself was coming to lecture at Strasbourg and Jean-Luc asked Philippe to pick him up at the train station. Philippe balked, saying Levinas would surely ask for an explication of Philippe's stance and he'd prefer not to confront him with his own difficult presence at the moment of arrival. Nonsense, Jean-Luc is to have retorted. Just go pick him up, he's not heard about your ostensible falling out yet, which you can elaborate patiently at the proper occasion. Plus the train station is just a few minutes' ride from the university. Philippe goes to pick up Levinas at the train station. It was a Friday afternoon, if I recall correctly. In any case there was a considerable traffic jam and they were stuck in the car. Levinas turns to Philippe saying he understands that they are in dispute. Would Philippe kindly explain himself. Horns are blaring, nothing's budging, Philippe finds himself obligated to respond to the great sage.

and when, ridesharing with Levinas in a traffic jam, they had all the time for Levinas to force him to say something. Stupefaction and cognition were often substitutable for Philippe, I realize, because taking the stance of not knowing or not understanding meant only that he understood all too well.

Still, when I once set out to provoke him in Berkeley, trying to stir trouble in my hysterical ingrate inexcusable betrayal kind of way—my style of responding shamelessly to the generosity and incomparable light of my friend—I told him that I had just read a passage in Paul de Man stating without frills or excuses that Lacoue-Labarthe had approached Nietzsche as a first-timer, with undisguised *naiveté*. Philippe reflected for a minute, maybe he blinked, and then said, simply: "that's not wrong." His probity was every time unimpeachable—no matter how hard I tried to find the loophole or to pry open a wounding dossier. He was in a way steady on his feet. "Don't be frightened because I have just pronounced this word: *philosophy*. It surely gives the appearance of being a big word, quite impressive. But philosophy itself, like everything else, is something that can be learned, a step at a time; and it's not as difficult as you may imagine. All you need to know, for starters is a couple of very simple things. And understand how they function. It's the beginning, as always, that's really important." Lacoue-Labarthe teaches the kids the names of the muses, the Greek origins of philosophical thought, and, for good measure, throws in some baby language theory. Reading along I consider how Philippe has offered my contemporaries and me, in Kleinian terms, "a good feed," a reassuring way to grasp the most recalcitrant of theoretical themes. I was thinking how in some respects, he had babied me intellectually—and he himself looked like a baby, I tell myself! He was such a baby, so world-class needy, but this is getting me off track.

What could this mean, that Lacoue-Labarthe babied some of his most earnest readers? Well, I recall how he took us through the toughest neighborhoods of questioning with unprecedented gentleness. He had a way of taking you by the hand as he cosseted fierce commentary. He had access to catastrophic insight and commanded a grammar of the mimetic hell to which we Westerners have been sent; yet, he operated these registers of knowing with discretion and calm. Maybe his statements didn't pass de Manian inspection because of the patterns of understated utterances of which he proved capable. There was a firm tonality but on the level of redescription he was at times unassuming, steady but modest, clear about his hesitations, reserved. For these reasons, I think, people have said, as if this could be calculated and judged absolutely—and maybe it can, I won't foreclose the possibility but make it instead a matter of taste—that they prefer Jean-Luc to Philippe. People had a tendency to say this, behind their backs and once or twice up in their faces. The split in tonalities wasn't hard to decode. Nancy dazzles and rips; Philippe keeps it low (which lets itself be confused with methodical, though I can't deny that he is at times methodical, crystal clear methodical); Jean-Luc takes risks, Philippe conceals his ever more subdued feats of risk-taking. Perhaps Philippe has invited implicit comparativity ever since he joined Jean-Luc after they decided, as they each told me on separate occasions, that they could not live apart, which is why they zoomed in on Strasbourg (where they were both hired by the same department, which could not have happened in Paris—this fact has led to speculation among a number of us about the fate of "French theory," how the cartography and emphasis might have changed if, for example, Jean-Luc had been stationed in some Paris university, then his reputation would have matched up strongly with that of Deleuze, long ago. If there were space for this, and I could indulge Derridean expanses, I would move now toward considerations of material mappings, surveying for instance what it meant that Heidegger refused to budge from home and cancelled the call from Berlin as he puts forth in his "Why We Remain in the Provinces," which I have more or less covered in good faith in the book *Stupidity*, or what we can make, on another level, of the transfers and homesteading of outstanding scholars from France to the United States, the waves that migrant intellectuals have created in academic history in terms of the yet uncharted displacements of Germans and Brits, Islanders, Argentineans, Africans, or what Derrida has criticized when we say "the rest of the world."

Philippe and Jean-Luc, in order to maintain their house of being stayed back in Strasbourg, where I, like so many, first met them before California became for a long while our shared haunt, and then lately we had spread to Paris and New York, while Jean-Luc remained in Strasbourg, practically commuting to Paris. But I have wanted to say something about Philippe's language of discretion, the firm ethicity of his gentle yet high impact articulations that changed the world for some of us, rendering thought in essential ways possible. He babied us, but only in the way that the reality principle goes after you and slaps you down from early on. Pampered, reality, pampered, reality: smack, smack. Philippe in some ways was an explorer of the possible, he rigorously remained on this side of facticity. So it may not be the Derridean impossibles that he took on, which is precisely what may have led Derrida himself to confront the work of Lacoue-Labarthe by entering into the vast registry of his philosophical and poetical reflections the thought of *désistance*. Philippe's work desists; it practices desistance rather than leaping off directly from the energies of resistance or outright language rebellion, the permanent insurrection to which we've become accustomed by Lyotard, Kofman, Cixous, and Deleuze. Still, the purported shift from resistance to desistance is more modulated and concealed than my description accounts for here—there is far more hesitancy and quasi-dialectical maneuvering around stated axioms of reluctance. The rhetorical flavor of desistance correlates, it seems to me, with Lacoue-Labarthe's native reserve and careful accounting, his nearly primal ethnicity, if such a clash of figures can be sustained. Desistance in the context of his writing, added on to the Heideggerian vocabulary of *Entfernung*, the withdrawal that *makes* itself, produces a non-negative turn or style, not far from the fateful phrasing of "I prefer not to." Derrida writes: "Without being negative, or being subject to a dialectic, [desistance] both organizes and disorganizes what it appears to determine." Lacoue-Labarthe, in any case, builds many key moves of his argument on the subtle propulsion of the *de-*, which Derrida situates as part of a hyperbologic characteristic of this oeuvre.

For my part, I suddenly realize, I have long lingered in the vicinity of the abyssal pull of such terms as *déconstitution, dépropriation*, as well as *disintallation* in Philippe's specific usage. Several courses that I gave in the Berkeley years, side by side with Philippe, were bound by the title and orientation "Depropriation," under which we studied the loss of the proper in a number of hyperventilating texts (Rousseau, Nietzsche, Bernhard), though some of them were quiet, calm, even passive about their disappropriating fatalities (Eckermann, Dickinson, Wheatley). About the dewords, Philippe was among the very few to stick up in *L'imitation des modernes*, for the oft discarded usage of "deconstruct"—a word that he does not consider "in the least 'worn out,'" but sees in it the pressure of a task, sometimes an imperative or event. I am winding down, now, I can feel it, pressured by page limits and other materialities—I have to reread everything, put it in some order, start writing up the columns and ledgers and vocabularies that in this numbed phase of shock are just swirling around, at random, in a disassociated way. Maybe I've followed the Hölderlinian path that much of Philippe's work depends on, the *ex-zentrische Bahn* or eccentric path, deviating from the start, off centering, for which any relation to this work calls. Or maybe I released myself to the custody of a haunting statement that he has made and that has captivated me ever since I first encountered it: Philippe links music, the musical drive, whether he means the blues or Wagner or "the rest of" his impressive contemporary repertory, with the autobiographical compulsion—a compulsion to speak, to tell, to venture even the unsayable. As a registered obsessional neurotic, I take my cues from such statements, they bind themselves to me as injunctions, forcing me to play them out, follow a score, even in bereaved *pianissimo*, quiet, quiet.

I didn't get to some of the children's questions in *Le chant des muses*. They ask him wonderfully aggressive, poignant, determined questions to which he responds with an exceptional grace, opening himself to another register of exposure. I recognize him in these moments, I can feel him breathing and smoking and looking out from his glasses, almost dumbfounded, by the stuporous request for knowledge. He was always there, even when confined to bed, to take our call. We have lost a friend, I tell myself, a world has gone down but what's left—"*was bleibet aber*"—is a certain rhythm to which he holds us, a still pulsing beat by which we hold him: Hölderlin, the Greeks, Nietzsche, Heidegger all acquired the dignity of a contemporary beat, an unheard of interlocution initiated and sustained by Philippe.

*The Tactlessness of an Unending Fadeout …*

> The gathering of recalling thought is not based on a
> human capacity, such as the capacity to remember and retain.
> All thinking that recalls what can be recalled in thought already
> lives in that gathering which beforehand has in its keeping
> and keeps hidden all that remains to be thought.
>
> MARTIN HEIDEGGER, *What is Called Thinking?*

In my uncertainty of attempting to respond to the call of mourning, to respond to mourning even though I had no certainty of not only whether I was doing so but more pertinently that I was attempting to do so whilst having no way of being certain what mourning was to begin with, I must have sent out a call. And my dear teacher and friend, Avital Ronell, must have picked up on my distress. For, she sent me her thoughts and her work of mourning, for and on Philippe Lacoue-Labarthe. And as I was voraciously pouring, almost tearing, through her work, in the hope—nearing desperation—of sinking my teeth into something that would guide me, help me, let me cling on to a particular certainty, what emerged from it was a certain calm, a certain friendship.

In attempting to attend to the voice of Philippe, her friendship with Philippe, in letting his thought foreground itself, thinking with him rather than for him, what occurred—is still occurring—was a resounding, a playful bouncing off, on and with each other, where there was a collision, a rebounding, a sounding of the two voices, both distinct, and yet never quite apart, resonating, reverberating without any attempt to be first—even though there was no choice but to be the one that is speaking, writing, for him, in his absence, in his memory, for his memory.

There was neither *prima donna* nor *primo uomo*; just music.

And what brought me some measure of comfort—even as it became more apparent that one can only mourn, that one perhaps only mourns whilst responding; thus never quite knowing what is calling one to mourn—was that writing, thinking, can be personal, warm, human.

—

As I dashed for help, one can never quite forget—keep out of one's mind—that in searching, in pleading, in asking, there is always a chance that one's hopes might be dashed. For, even if the call is answered, even if the other attempts to attend to it, there is no, never any, guarantee that the response might have anything to do with the call. In some way, a call for, call to, a calling, and its response, might always be separated by a dash—

But it is not as if this dash, this cut, caesura, is absolute as well: it is also a connection to another, the other, a point of touch. And here, we can never forget that in order to touch there has to be some distance—if we are too close, in the same place, we are already consuming, subsuming, the other, one another.

Do we only dash to another if there is something in them, an element in them, of them—even and perhaps especially if this element remains veiled—that we find dashing?

—

A register of the call that cannot be ignored, even as much as one may wish to, is its potentially accusatory nature. For, one is called by something, someone; and more precisely, one is called to answer (that very call itself). Here, we can hear an echo of one being called to the stand, being called to stand, being called to testify to something, someone; and there is no reason why this testimony is not of one's very self. In being called to testify, one could also be called to defend—in being called to the stand, one could well be defending an accusation. In standing against that accusation, one could be called to answer for a crime that one didn't even commit in the first place; a crime that one is now compelled to answer for because one had had the gumption (or it might have been instinctive, un-thought, accidental even) to answer the call.

Here, we catch a glimpse of the problem K. faces in *The Trial*: whether he had actually committed the crime or not is unknown (and perhaps unimportant); what is more crucial is that he is called to answer, account for, a crime, and more precisely a crime that he remains blind to. After all, it is not as if one does not break the law numerous times each day—the trouble is that in attempting to account for a crime that remains veiled from us, we inadvertently end up admitting to even more crimes. Perhaps anything that we say, or do, can be used against us.

So, even as we are attempting to answer, we might actually be confessing, opening ourselves to even more accusations as we try to respond. And here we might recall Hélène Cixous' recollection in *Portrait of Jacques Derrida as a Young Jewish Saint*, where she meditates on the paradox that is a confession: "Here I should recall why we confess to God who knows, *cur confitemur Deo scienti*, why we only truly confess ourselves to God-who-knows because He knows it is not a question of knowing; and on condition: on condition there is no other witness than God-who-knows, on condition we make our confession to no one other than God, therefore to No One, to God-who-knows-as-likewise-He-does-not-know, to God the Ear for my word, God as my very own Ear into which, out my silence, I thrust my avowal, aloud, in order to hear myself and (not) be heard by anyone else (other than God)."[1] [This is especially true since the very person we are speaking to, speaking for, responding to, is already dead, already knows that (s)he is dead—our testimony of her life is about her, and also never for her; (s)he is the last person that needs our testimony; it is her life, and (s)he is the one that has led it, knows more about it than the one who is uttering, testifying.] For, if you both have to know (to confess), and cannot know (who you are confessing to) at the same time, not only is it always a leap of faith since the object of confession is not as important as the fact that one is confessing, all confession is no longer in the realm of truth-falsity. By confessing, one is doing nothing but testifying to the fact one is confessing. And moreover, one can only testify if one is unsure of the facts (otherwise no testimony is needed). And since the testimony comes through you—another cannot testify on your behalf—one has no real choice but to narrate one's testimony; bringing with it all the problems of forgetting, and ultimately, fictionality.

In speaking, is one confessing the need to confess, confessing the very inadequateness of one's confession, confessing that one has no means to address the one who is lying there other than by confessing?

In confessing, is what is being confessed the very notion of confession itself? After all, it is not as if the penance ever matches—or was even intended

---

[1] Hélène Cixous. *Portrait of Jacques Derrida as a Young Jewish Saint*. trans. Beverly Bie Brahic. (New York: Columbia University Press), 2004: 48.

to match—the sin confessed. It is an act of contrition, a rite; and what is being confessed is what is being confessed—*what I have said, I have said.*

> *"For those whose sins you forgive, they are forgiven; for those whose sins you retain, they are retained." —John* 19:23

This opens the question of whether there is an unconfessable act (leaving aside the nature of this act itself). This is not the same question of whether the confession is pardonable, forgivable. In a way, this question comes before that: for, without a confession, there can be no opening for forgiveness. Which is not to say that it is a matter of phases, procedure—if that were so, forgiveness would be reduced to a mere function; an affect to a cause. And in many instances, a confession and the call for forgiveness come almost simultaneously, as if the call were already part of the confession itself. This suggests that the confessibility of an act has little to nothing to do with the result—response even—to the confession. We could claim that the onus lies solely on the confessor—but this would not be completely true, too; one can only "truly confess to [someone] who already knows." And this opens the register that one can only confess if the other is also willing to hear one's confession—perhaps regardless of whether there is, or eventually will be, forgiveness involved.

But what happens when this other is also dead?

how do I mourn thee?

Not you, for that would remind me too much of a you, a person—not a person as such but one in relation with all others, every other. But thee, a personal, one that is just one as one, singular.

But since you are gone, the one that I am attempting to mourn is always already in my memory, remembered. Which fragment of you have I resurrected? Is it even possible to speak of thee as such any longer? Or perhaps it is this fragmented, fragmentary, nature of the remembrance that ensures every memory is singular. Not that I am necessarily able to tell the difference between them. For, each recollection of thee, you, is haunted by the possibility of forgetting. And since there is no object to forgetting, no referentiality—all I can possibly articulate is the fact that I might have forgotten—there is no possibility of knowing what is being forgotten. There is no possibility of knowing if each time one remembers, each moment of memory might bring with it forgetting as well. In other words, forgetting is not always in an antonymic relationality with memory, both are possibly a part of each other.

Not only can I not know if my resurrection of thee is accurate, it might not even have anything to do with thee. It might be a you—not just in relation with all others, every other, but a you that is completely other.

Perhaps all I can mourn is the possibility of thee.

Perhaps all that allows me to mourn in the first place is the possibility that I have forgotten, am always forgetting, thee.

Perhaps then, all I can mourn is you.

Any act of memory, any recalling, is an attempt to respond to something which, someone who has, left a trace in one. Here, it is not too difficult to hear an echo of the eternal request, that of "do this in memory of me." This opens the register of *what kind of memory is one being asked to recall*? For, it is not as if Jesus of Nazareth did not have a notion of how he would have liked to be remembered by his disciples: the trouble is that none of them were—or could ever be—privy to that particular notion. This was most clearly seen in the vastly different reaction of Judas Iscariot from the other eleven at the scene of the request. What this calls into question is the notion of the relationality between the author and the reader; of whether the author has any control over what the reader reads, is reading, has read.

It is not difficult to hear an echo of authority in author; as if the writer of the situation can play at being God—all-seeing, and in full control. The trouble with authority is that it is always already illegitimate. For, if something is legitimate, access to it would be open to everyone—governed by a universal Law. It is only when something is illegitimate that the authority of a person is required to enact it. For instance, a death-sentence can only be pardoned by the authority of the sovereign. In doing so (s)he is going against the legal system which sentenced that person to death; the same legal system that upholds her very sovereignty. In other words, authority is the very undoing of the Law. However, a foregrounding of the illegitimacy of the sovereign would not only shatter the illusion, but also bring about the collapse of the entire system. After all, it is not as if one can read without the figure of the author: even if one posits that the author is dead, a spectral presence—even as a fiction, perhaps especially as a fiction—has to be maintained; otherwise the fantasy of the text that can be approached, that can possibly be read, crumbles. The very source of that authority—of why someone has authority, and more than that, why we grant authority to someone, thereby necessitating our subjectification to that figure who only has the authority due to our self-subjectification—remains outside of reason, remains unknown; remains a secret.

After all, it is not as if we can ever know what "me" is.

We should remember that this statement takes place in the scene of trans-substantiation. And this reopens the register of remembering and forgetting: for, this is a process where there is a change in substance of the bread and wine (into the body and blood of Christ), but one which the senses are not privy to. In other words, this is change in substance, but one in which there is no referentiality; and this unverifiable, and ultimately illegitimate, trans-substantiation is only possible due to the potentiality of forgetting. For, if memory was complete—if one could know for sure—then by extension, possibility is governed by correspondence: the fact that we can never be sure, that we can never control forgetting, suggests the possibility of changes occurring whilst remaining exterior to our cognition, to our scope of knowing. But here we must go even further and examine what occurs even when there is the possibility of referentiality.

In order to do so, we have to consider what it means to say '_____ is like _____', that 'something is like something else'; for, the statement of relationality is the very basis of all correspondence. Whenever one utters '_____ is like _____', there is always already the echo of preference that haunts the statement; that this relationality is uttered only because the one who utters it wants it to be so. Whether it is a biased statement or not is irrelevant; what is crucial is the fact that this statement would not exist— this relationality would not be—if it were not called into being by that person. However, in order for the person to call this relationality into being, (s)he would have to first assume the possibility of this very relationality itself; it is only retrospectively that the validity of the statement '_____ is like _____' can be tested. Hence, this is a statement that is based on nothing but the assumption of the possibility that '_____ is like _____'. In other words, this statement of relationality is not a statement of reference, of correspondence, but the very naming of referentiality itself: in order to make the statement, one must first assume the possibility of referentiality; and the statement '_____ is like _____' is its very name. In terms of reading, each time one reads, one is opening a connection to the other, and more specifically naming the very possibility of this connection itself. As Avital Ronell reminds us, "the connection to the other is a reading—not an interpretation, assimilation, or even a hermeneutic understanding, but a reading."[1] Each time you "do this in memory of me," you are doing nothing but reading—attempting to read—what "me" is.

---

[1] Avital Ronell. *The Telephone Book: Technology, Schizophrenia, Electric Speech*. (Lincoln: University of Nebraska Press), 1989: 380.

[We should try not to forget that the term *like* comes from *lich*, which etymologically can be traced to corpse. Here, one might open the register that we call the *oeuvre* of an author her *body of work*. One should note, though, that etymologically speaking, there is no specific mention of the body in the term: it traces itself back to *opus*, or work. Hence, the *body* that we are referring to might well be that of the author—the work that is written on her self. Perhaps, then, the "me" that we are asked to remember is not only the text to be read, it is also the text that is being written each time we are attempting to read it. For, it is not as if we are privy to the author, to the authoring, of that text. It is not as if we can ever tell if it is we who are authoring as we are reading, or even if there was an authoring: perhaps the authoring is precisely in the reading of the text.

One might even consider the fact that this scene happens twice—once with the body, and once with the blood. Perhaps there is always already the recognition that there is more than one memory, there is more than one "me" to be remembered. And even if they are contrasting, complementary, perhaps contradictory, memories, they form part of a "me" that can never (at least with any certainty) be whole. Here, we might go further and speculate that it is precisely the duality of the situation that is crucial: if there is only one, single, "me" to be remembered, once this happens, all need for memory is over—it is only the duality, the potential uncertainty, the duel in, and of, memories that maintains the need to "do this in memory of me."]

We might also want to consider what kind of statement "do this in memory of me" is. If it is an order, this reopens our considerations of the Law. For, if it is an imperative from Jesus of Nazareth, and his disciples are not privy to the intent of his command, they are facing a situation where they are affected by a Law, one which has effects on them, but which they remain blind to. Hence, each attempt to respond to his command is one where they are stumbling around in the dark. If we posit that it is a request, that doesn't change the fact that none of the twelve know what they are responding to: what is opened though is the notion that Jesus of Nazareth already pre-empts the possibility that they were going to forget him the moment he was dead. [One might claim that the only reason the Nazarene had to command them to "do this in memory of me" is that he knew they would otherwise forget him.] What is perhaps more interesting is if we consider the notion that Jesus of Nazareth knows that forgetting him is inevitable: that all they could possibly have is a certain memory of him. In this way, "do this in memory of me" is a soft plea. And more than that, it is a remembering of him that has to take place through a ritual. For, rituals are meaningless: but it is precisely through set gestures, a series of rites, that his disciples might be able to resurrect a particular, singular, memory—different each time—of him. And it is in this manner that he is able to live, not by cheating death, but precisely by dying. It is only due to the fact that his disciples forget him that Jesus of Nazareth is able to die to live.

But it is not as if even a ritual will allow us to respond to a memory in full; not that we can even know what a full memory is. Remembering only ever occurs in exception to memory—quite possibility in betrayal of a memory. In this way, each remembrance is a naming of that memory, a naming of something as memory, bringing with it an act of violence, especially since there is no basis to the naming except for the naming. Each time one names, one is picking one name over every other name; privileging one name whilst all other(s) are marginalized. However, this is a violence that is not an effacement as there is no claim to the validity of this naming; this is precisely because each act of naming is a tautological gesture, one that makes no claim to reason, to logic, to truth, but remains in the realm of *doxa*, opinion.

Even though it is of *doxa*, one cannot do away with the fact that each naming is a betrayal of all other names. If anything, it might actually increase it: after all, if there is no *Grund*, one is choosing a particular path, making a certain decision, based on nothing but the fact that one is.

As I attempt to mourn thee, even if I can mourn only you, I have no choice but to name you, give the mourning a name. At the same time, in choosing to mourn thee, I have to betray thee—in memory of thee.

*how do I mourn thee?*

stories … names

> "Before you die you're a bastard. After that, you're a fucking saint ..."
> —MAURICE JAMES BEINS

How is one supposed to write a eulogy for a man who opens a challenge to the very premise of all eulogies? For, eulogies are a *discourse of praise*, wherein one is supposed to only utter good words about someone; as if in their absence they can do no wrong. And perhaps it is this that he so succinctly captures: it is only because the person is now absent that (s)he can do no wrong. In this sense, the term "living saint" can only be an oxymoron—even as a figure of speech, it tends to be applied only to persons that are not actually in our vicinity; and they usually are people that we don't, or at least hardly, even know.

One might even posit that it is because we don't know them that we can say only good things about them—the more one knows someone, even if we take into consideration all the problems of knowing, the greater the likelihood of encountering something about them that we dislike, quite possibly for no other reason than taste, or bias. Hence, in order to eulogise someone, one has no choice but to adopt a deliberate blindness towards the person, towards aspects of what makes that person a person. In other words, we have to adopt a particular distance when we are making a *priori* selections of that person.

In order to eulogise, we have to first make the person not only an object (one that we can dissect, separate neatly), we also have to make her a stranger.

At the very least, this opens a register on friendship—specifically a type of friendship that is needed in order to write a eulogy. For, it both requires a closeness, a familiarity, and at the same time a particular kind of separation from the friend. And this reopens a thinking of a kind of betrayal that is needed for a eulogy—where one has to betray a certain side of a friend in order to be their friend. Here, we can hear an echo of Plutarch, who in the opening of his biography *Alexander the Great* writes, "it must be borne in mind that my design is not to write histories, but lives."[1] One can immediately detect his

---

[1] Plutarch. *The Life of Alexander the Great*. trans. John Dryden. (New York: The Modern Library), 2004: 3.

distinction between writing lives, which composes of particular narratives with their underlying tropes, from an attempt an to encompass, master, a multiplicity of tales, some of which would be contrary to what he is trying to convey. But perhaps what is more important to us here (at the risk of a Plutarchian gesture whilst commenting on him) is Plutarch's acknowledgment of his role in writing the biography, that the Alexander of *Alexander the Great* is his.

One could, of course, see it as an effacing gesture, even an arrogant one: as if the writer's perspective is more important than the reality of the life one is writing on, about. However, if we consider the notion that reality always already escapes us, slips all attempts to capture, eludes knowing—reopening echoes of the illegitimacy of authorship—does the writer have any choice but to enact a particular violence whilst writing? Moreover, reality itself implies a certain grasping, seizing, of some parts, certain particularities—whilst ceasing, enacting a *caesura* on, others. In this sense, by foregrounding his role as the author, Plutarch is acknowledging a responsibility not only towards his text, but also to Alexander himself—by recognizing, accepting, that there is a particular purpose in telling these particular tales; eulogising Alexander as the great one.

The trouble, though, is that one can only write: whether whatever is written is read, or heard, as praise is a completely different matter. As Alberto Manguel reminds us in his text on his friend Jorge Luis Borges, even with the best of intentions, "even in the realm of friendship, the role of the reader predominates. The reader, not the writer."[2]

For, one can only write in an attempt to write. Writing comes to one—from somewhere else, everywhere else, anywhere else; often in spite of one self. Hence, even as all writing can only happen through the self, the self is—and can only be—the medium through which it occurs. The only thing that one can do is attempt to respond, attend, to the possibility of writing itself. By being in front of a keyboard, by having a notebook on me. By reading. All craft

---

[2] Alberto Manguel. *With Borges.* (London: Telegram Books), 2006: 60.

is a form of mimesis; and writing often begins with reading something, anything. After which one might be able to form a certain relationality between what is read and what is being written. But it is not as if every mimesis is writing. Even though there is no verifiable difference between a grammatically correct sentence and a piece of writing, one can only know the difference the moment it is read, perhaps only at the point of reading itself.

Being open to possibilities means that one has to concede that one is never quite in control of one's thoughts, one's writing. Sometimes, whatever is written is strange, unfamiliar, other, to one—a fragment of one.

And since one can never quite control how it will be read, one can only write, read, and leave it to be read.

Which opens the possibility that whenever one is attempting to write a eulogy, it might always already be written for one self; and more specifically the self in one that is one's own reader. For, as Jacques Derrida so poignantly reflects in his eulogy for Roland Barthes: "he will receive nothing of what I say here of him, for him, to him, beyond the name but still within it, as I pronounce his name that is no longer his. This living attention here comes to tear itself towards that which, or the one who, can no longer receive it; it rushes towards the impossible. But if his name is no longer his, was it ever? I mean simply, uniquely?"[3]

So, even as we write-speak a discourse of praise in his name, what continues to haunt the discourse is his very name; and whether the name that is uttered in the very attempt to eulogise him is even his name any longer. Hence, not only do we have to take up the position of stranger yet friend, more pertinently, we end up having to cast him as a stranger to himself; his very own name only highlights the fact that it is no longer him that we are speaking of. "When I say Roland Barthes it is certainly him whom I name, him beyond his name. But since he himself is now inaccessible to this appellation, since

---

[3] Jacques Derrida. *The Work of Mourning*. trans. Pascale-Anne Brault and Michael Nass. (Chicago: University of Chicago Press), 2003: 45.

this nomination cannot become a vocation, address, or apostrophe (supposing that this possibility revoked today could have ever been pure), it is him in me that I name, toward him in me, in you, in us that I pass through his name. What happens around him and is said about him remains between us. Mourning began at this point. But when? For even before the unqualifiable event called death, interiority (of the other in me, in you, in us) had already begun its work."[4]

In saying "Maurice James Beins," I have no choice but to name him in spite of the impossibility of naming him; in saying his name, I am naming the fact that it is impossible to name him. Perhaps all that I am naming is the fact that ever since I have known his name, I have been doing nothing but preparing to name him; in preparing to name him, I have been doing nothing but starting to mourn the day where there is nothing I can do but say his name.

And since I can only say his name, even as his name is other to me, and potentially to himself, this suggests that we can only utter his name as a citation to himself. In other words, "Maurice James Beins"—as in the case of "Roland Barthes"—is a quotation to himself, even as much as the referentiality of this citation remains unstable.

Here, we might momentarily want to keep in mind the potential question that accompanies all citation, all quotations: is one choosing a quotation, a thinker, a kind of thinking, because one likes it, because it happens to suit one at that particular moment? This opens various registers of citationality: whether we are citing to pay a certain homage, an acknowledgement that the thought comes from another, from elsewhere; whether we are deferring to another; whether that moment of deference brings with it a shielding of ourselves, as if to say, *if you have an issue with that thought, don't argue with me; pick your fight with the other.* By uttering the name of the person we are attempting to praise, are we always already shielding our utterances, our selves, with his name?

---

[4] *Ibid.*: 46.

And even as we are attempting to consider the notion of preference—even to guard against it for fear that biasness may cloud our thinking—we cannot turn a blind eye to the fact that there are effects on our corporeal being, perhaps even affecting our very thinking. For, even as we may be attempting to fortify ourselves as we pay homage, praise, to the person, we cannot escape the fact that it is us who not only pick the particular stories to tell, it is also our very self who is selecting this name to be uttered.

In other words, even as these utterances are taking place in the form of a eulogy—with its specific rules and form regarding what we should say—these utterances themselves are not entirely divorced from us.

And if one invokes the notion of form, of what can or cannot be in a eulogy, one has to also evoke the notion of precedence, of all the eulogies that have come before us. Here, it is not difficult to hear an echo of a phrase that we have been using rather regularly in the last few minutes; that of "in other words." This opens the question of exactly whose words are we using here: since the narrative of a eulogy is usually deemed to correspond with, to, the life of the person, these are his words, even as their referentiality remains in question. This remains a question not in a sense of did he say—or write—them (that would be fairly easy to verify, even though one must never forget the entire history of mis-attributions that haunt the legitimacy of citations), but rather, every citation, attribution, is always already out of context. In this sense, whenever we say "in other words," we are not only pointing out the fact that these are not exactly our words, we are also covering, veiling, the notion that these are precisely our words—if not in content, then surely in form, in sequence—words that are ordered according to our needs, desires. Hence, we are once again unable to do away with one of our initial concerns: the notion of bias, preference. In creating a particular *corpus*—and here we reopen the register of relationality, likeness, bodies—are we always already writing our own bodies into it: by evoking the name of whom we eulogise, by resurrecting him through a séance of language—by playing medium here—am I always already injecting, inseminating, my self into that dissemination? And it is no coincidence that the conventional sign of citation—quotation marks—are occasionally referred to as *vampire marks*—not only do they look like puncture wounds, whenever one quotes one is enacting a violence of context by abducting—dragging—out of context. More than that, one is also appropriating the life, the force (by way of its effects), the energy, of the words, for one's own purposes.

In other words—for what choice do I have here but to foreground the otherness in what I am attempting to say—whatever I am saying, even as much as I am attempting to legitimise through, and with, the other, is always already haunted by the spectre of illegitimacy. For, even as one—I—is attempting to *back up* what is said with others, I—one—am never able to distinguish which are my—one's—words, from that of the other. Hence, it is not just that one is unable to tell one self from the other, both one and the other are now also potentially indivorceable.

And here, if we momentarily reopen the register that all knowledge is a form of memory, this suggests that all that we know is a citation, a quotation. Since we can never do away with the possibility of forgetting, we will not only be uncertain of our knowledge, of what we know, we will also never quite know whether what we know is from us, or from another. As Hélène Cixous reminds us, "citation is the voice of the other and it highlights the double playing of the narrative authority. We constantly hear the footsteps of the other, the footsteps of others in language, others speaking in Stephen's language or in Ulysses', I mean in the book's language … It reminds us that we have been caught up in citation ever since we said the first words mama or papa."[5] In other words, each utterance, every attempt to speak, write, brings with it the notion of otherness. Hence, the very stability of the *I* is always already called into question. The self and the other can no longer be seen as antonyms. Not only is the self and the other in relation with each other, the self is potentially other to itself. The potential uncertainty grows if we take into consideration the teaching of Paul de Man, who never lets us forget that "it is impossible to say where quotation ends and 'truth' begins, if by truth we understand the possibility of referential

---

[5] Hélène Cixous. *Stigmata*. (London: Routledge), 2005: 135.

verification. The very statement by which we assert that the narrative is rooted in reality can be an unreliable quotation; the very document, the manuscript, produced in evidence may point back not to an actual event, but to an endless chain of quotations reaching as far back as the ultimate transcendental signified God, none of which can lay claim to referential authority."[6] In this manner, it is impossible to distinguish a moment of reading from a potential re-writing. And since reading and writing are haunted by illegitimacy—both ultimately lacking any necessary referent—all reading is a potential writing (which can only happen if all writing is also a reading of sorts).

In other words, not only is the name of the other—the name of "Maurice James Beins"—other to himself, one's words are also always already potential other to oneself.

And if one is ultimately unable to distinguish between reading and re-writing, one can never legitimise one's eulogy. At best, all one can say is, "what I have written, I have written."

"Quod scripsi, scripsi." PONTIUS PILATE, *John* 22:19

Why the double statement? Why the need to reinforce—shouldn't once be enough, especially when it is coming from an official of the Roman Empire? Does one repeat when one is sure, when one reinforces the fact that one is sure, or does it also open a question on one's own certainty; where the second half is an attempt to reassure both the listener, and perhaps more pertinently the one who utters, of the legitimacy of what he has written, what I have written. One cannot divorce what Pilate has written from the law: after all, what he writes is the law—the Nazarene is indeed King because of his statement, "*Iesus Nazarenus, Rex Iudaeorum*." Here, one can reopen the register that Pilate is the author of the law, bringing with it all the illegitimacy of authoring, authority; that he is indeed writing the law as he is reading it.[7] One might also speculate why

---

[6] Paul de Man. *Allegories of Reading: Figural Language in Rousseau, Nietzsche, Rilke, and Proust.* (New Haven: Yale University Press), 1979: 204.

he chooses to focus on the fact that he has written it. Even though the legal form requires a written aspect, the foregrounding of writing in his utterance opens a consideration of "*Iesus Nazarenus, Rex Iudaeorum*" being a truth that he could write, but not speak. For, if this were a dangerous truth—one cannot ignore the fact that he was in Jerusalem, and the notion that the Nazarene was their King was not exactly a popular one—then it is curious that it is recorded, in writing, permanent, as opposed to uttered, and potentially transient. Here though, we might want to consider the notion that utterances, speech, highlight the presence of the elocutioner; one is conversely always able to take a certain distance towards what is written—Pilate is, in fact, able to claim that he is merely repeating, recording, the words of the Nazarene himself; words from a response that was an echo of his own words, that of "it is you who say I am." In a way, Pilate's writing is a recording of a loop—a remix if you will—of a title that is bounced back and forth between himself and Jesus of Nazareth.

[Here, let us risk a side-track, and tune into the role of DJ Pontius Pilate. In recording a remixed version of the response of the Nazarene, he opens it up to reading. This is not to say that speech does not need to be read, but there is a lower likelihood that the Pharisees were going to directly question the pronouncement of a Roman official. Once written for all to see, though, one could claim to be seeking clarification on a hermeneutical level—this we see when the chief priests said to Pilate: "You should not write 'King of the Jews', but rather, 'this man said: I am King of the Jews'"[8]—or even clarity for the writer himself, when he re-reads what he has written. However, in opening his

---

[7] Take for instance a situation at a pedestrian light-controlled intersection. A policeman who has seen you crossing the road whilst the light turns red mid-way can summon you both for not stopping, and also for stopping. Either way, you are infringing the law. This is true even though the law itself is not consistent. For, there are basically two lights—green to signal "go," and red to signal "stop." The problem lies in the fact that "green" is an invitation (one can choose to walk, or not to, whenever green is showing), whilst 'red' is an order, an imperative (when the red light is on, one has no choice but to stop). To compound matters, if one is crossing the road (whilst the light is green, so no law is being broken) and the light suddenly turns to red, one cannot stop—in fact, at that point, the thing to do is to run like hell. Hence, sometimes one is required to break the law in order to follow the law. However, the policeman is the absolute arbiter in this case. So, not only does (s)he read your actions to determine if you have followed the law or not, (s)he is also the writer of the law as (s)he is judging you by the very law that (s)he has just written.

[8] *John* 19:20-22.

words to reading, DJ PP was also opening it to variations, all of them potentially different, perhaps even contradictory: the mix-tapes of the chief priests, the people, the disciples of the Nazarene, all possibly had nothing to do with each other. Which is not to say that each reading affects them any less, nor are the effects any less on the DJ himself. For, as (s)he is writing, (s)he is selecting, picking, as if conducting an orchestra—where all the musicians, instruments, tones—are possibilities of words, letters, combinations, limited only by her imagination, her creation, and also a set of rules, laws, grammar; the same limitations that the reader, (s)he as her reader, is governed by. And as (s)he is playing with these possibilities, so are the readers, so is (s)he as her own other.

Writing—spinning—mixing—reading.

And when one hears writing, if one listens carefully, one can also pick up on a certain writhing, a slipping, sliding, slithering, in, and with, language. And here, one might reopen speculation on the uncomfortable relationality between authority and authorship; and the writer having to sneak herself in, not just past the reader, but past herself as reader, her reading of herself.]

This brings us back once again to the repetition, to the double, to the return of the same. But what return? We might even venture further and wonder: what was Pilate wishing would return? Considering the situation he was in, a colonial ruler surrounded by people who were only turning to him in order that they could crucify Jesus of Nazareth—encircled by those who usually regarded him as the enemy—it is quite plausible that all he wanted was for the entire ordeal to be over. For, there is a hint of resignation in his tone, a certain weariness in the repetition, a repletion of his will: almost a plea for everyone to stop questioning him. One might also consider the notion of the realm of questioning being beyond that of the chief priests' enquiry of the validity of Pilate's statement: it is not inconceivable that the writer himself was having doubts about what was surely an unusual statement on his part. It is also possible to detect an inflection of a question in the second half of "what I have written, I have written"; not in a hermeneutical sense, but more pertinently *did I really write that*? For, there was no way in which Pilate—or anyone—could have verified that Jesus of Nazareth was the King of the Jews: it was based on nothing but the response of Jesus to an accusation from Pilate himself. In other words, it was a statement based on a claim that was never even made—if it came from anywhere, it was from somewhere other to both Pilate and Jesus. And if indeed Pilate was responding to a call from elsewhere, this was a response to a call that only he was privy to; which might be why after he had written what he had written, he was immediately faced with outrage. This might be why the statement was tautological: Pilate was actually saying nothing in the repetition besides the fact that he was saying something—it was a only a response to the question from the chief priest in form. There are echoes of Nietzsche here, in particular his teaching that the return of the same is rarely, if ever, exactly the same; perhaps only in form. So, even as Pilate was repeating himself, there was always already the possibility of something exterior to himself in that response, something that even he was not aware of, privy to. In other words, the response might well have been for someone, or something, other to the chief priests; perhaps even other to himself. Which reopens the possibility of Pilate responding in writing to a call from powers beyond him: after all, the only way in which one can communicate with the divine is through a medium; symbolically, ritualistically.

And this returns us again to the question of writing, of eulogies, and the notion of a dedication. For, even as Pilate was probably inscribing the sign in relation to Jesus of Nazareth, there was always already the possibility that it spoke with, and to, more. Even as we—I—write a eulogy with a person in mind, I—we—am potentially addressing something other to whom we are attempting to address.

The question that remains with us, that arises, that perhaps is raised as it is the one left behind, is: as the one remaining, how are we able to write that eulogy for the one who goes, the one who leaves us behind? This is a question not so much of *will (s)he receive the eulogy, this testimony (even though it is an important and prevalent thought)*, but one of *can one even testify about another*—can one testify for anyone but another? Does one have to be able to comprehend the issue at hand in order to be a witness to it; does one have to know in order to witness? And in all of these, there are two factors at play: the ability to comprehend, to see, to understand; and the notion of an active role, that of choice in testimony, choosing to testify. As Jacques Derrida reminds us, one of the difficulties of testifying is that, "testimony always goes hand in hand with at least the *possibility* of fiction, perjury, and the lie. Were this possibility to be eliminated, no testimony would be possible any longer; it could no longer have the meaning of testimony."[9] But in order to begin to even contemplate the notion of lies, fiction, and possible untruths, we have to first address a more basic question, that of *what exactly are we are attempting to testify to?*; which is a question of uncertainty towards the very thing we are witnessing. This is crucial as it affects the very basis of one's ability to witness. For, in order to respond, one must first respond to the notion of one's relationality with the object of one's response. And hence, all witnessing is always already haunted by the question of hermeneutics; at some point all witnessing is subject to the question of what does this event that I am witnessing mean? In any attempt to witness, one is left with one's version of the event—in other words, all one can offer is one's interpretive gesture. Even if there are others around, the only solace they can give is their own interpretations. The event that one is bearing witness to is always already past, recalled, called forth, through the very act of testifying to it, subject to the subject's memories, along with all the uncertainty it brings. In this manner, witnessing is not so much a gesture of truth or falsity: one is ultimately making utterances without any possibility of referentiality, without any possibility of knowing whether one is right or not. One is attempting to respond to a situation with nothing but the fact that one is witnessing. This suggests that every testimony, every act of witnessing, is an act of inscribing, an act of writing, narrating. More specifically, it is an act of narrating in the first person; for, one can only witness for oneself. And since the narrator has to be present at the event in order to narrate, there is always already the problem of indiscernability at play; of whether the *I* of the first person narrative refers to the narrator of the tale, or the character that is in the tale. And it is the impossibility of differentiating them at any given moment that continually haunts

---

[9] Jacques Derrida. *Demeure: Fiction and Testimony.* trans. Elizabeth Rottenberg. (Stanford: Stanford University Press), 2000: 27.

every testimony. Hence, every act of witnessing, every act of testifying, is always already inscribed with the unknowability of whether the witness is recounting a tale, or telling it; whether the witness is narrating the tale or telling it as a character in the tale. For, a narrator would know the entire tale before recounting it; a character only knows what is happening at the point it is happening. And it is the indistinguishability of the two that leaves the testimony unaware of its own status: of whether each utterance is constative or performative. Not only is anyone hearing the testimony unable to be certain of the verifiability of what (s)he is hearing, the testifier herself is also blind to her own testimony.

The only thing that might be clear is that an attempt, any attempt, to testify is caught in an aporia: one can only respond if one knows what one is responding to, but at the same time one is unsure—can never be sure—about what one is responding to. As Jacques Derrida elegantly testifies, this is the "distinction between fiction and autobiography that not only remains undecidable but, far more serious, in whose indecidability, as de Man makes clear, it is impossible to *stand*, to maintain oneself in a stable or stationary way. One thus finds oneself in a fatal and double impossibility: the impossibility of deciding, but the impossibility of *remaining* in the undecidable."[10] In testifying, all one can do is testify, even in the impossibility of doing so; narrate one's tale, keeping in mind the fact that one is absolutely responsible; as all one is doing, all one is able to do, is name the event, bringing with it all the problems of a name. For, a name is a referent, with all the spectres of its history, its own stories, its own tales; at the same time it is always already illegitimate as there is no reason anything is named as such except for the fact that it is named such. Each name is always already tautological, referring to nothing except itself, except to the fact that it is so; and at the same time, to an entire history, to everything else except itself. Hence, each testimony, each naming, is a foregrounding of itself as a catachrestic metaphor; where the testifier is faced with "the impossibility of deciding [the name], but the impossibility of remaining in the undecidable," where the testifier cannot name, but has to name.

---

[10] *Ibid.*: 16.

To compound matters, in eulogies, in testifying to the event of the passing, to the absence of the object of one's witnessing, one has no choice but to use the person's name. In naming the person, not only are questions of whether one is able to encompass the life of a person in a name, or whether it is adequate for a name to remember the person, opened—more pertinently, it is a also a name for a particular future. For, each time we call something, recall something, it has to be from a past; otherwise we can not do so: one cannot call to mind something that is absolutely unknown to one. However, each recollection is always already a reconstitution, a re-writing, a re-vision as well: hence, it is also an event that has not yet happened, it is also an event that is to come. In effect, each time an event is called to mind, each time the name of an event is uttered, it is the moment where all time comes together; the event is present but only insofar as the present is a future anterior moment.

This is no longer just a question of hermeneutics—the meaning(s) of both testimony, and the object of our testimony—but more pertinently a calling into question of the relationality between the testifier, and her testimony.

As one reads the text—attempts to read the life of the person—as one is writing a text in response to the text, is one always already framing it, not just in the sense of setting a boundary, limit, border, and giving it a particular shape, but more pertinently, accusing it of, setting it up for, something that (s)he might not even have done; framing her for a life that is not even hers to begin with? In writing of her, one is in the realm of biography, of inscribing the *bios* of the person—always keeping in mind that *graphein* is of the order of permanence, fixity; of death. And if we take into account that one's bios is of the order of the social, the political (and not bare life, *zoē*), we must then take responsibility for the particular perception of her life that we are writing, that we are condemning to death, even as we are attempting to resurrect a certain memory of her. In resuscitating a certain memory, are we also framing her in that very way, condemning her to a particular frame: we should remember that a eulogy is often the last way in which people will hear of her, the last light in which she will be seen. And here, we have to reopen the register of the illegitimacy of authorship: in exerting the authority that every author, any author, has to—one has no choice but to do so in order to write, speak—one is doing so without any validity whatsoever. In that manner, even if one is trying one's utmost to respond to the life of the person, even if one is reading her as a response, trying to play detective with absolute rigour, care, respect, one can never be sure if one is discovering something about, or only unveiling the very clues that one has written, inseminated, as one is reading. [It is of no coincidence that in the classic Hollywood thriller, the detective must throw in her badge—turn away from the law—in order to begin her true work, her actual finding. Whilst this could suggest that being *beyond the pale* and justice might not always be antonymic, one cannot deny that a detective is always potentially in the realm of criminality: after all, most of the crimes are solved only when the detective resorts to breaking the law to obtain the crucial piece of evidence.] Each reading, each writing, of the person, on her life, even if only temporal, provisional, is a momentary conviction—one that is made without any possible legitimacy; at best only *beyond reasonable doubt*.

[Each time you eulogise, its rules always already bind you. As you take the stand, you are taking a stance, mounting the final defense for, of, the person, for her—you are her defense attorney and you are delivering a, her, *discourse of praise*. Those in front of you, potentially hearing, reading—perhaps even listening—to you, to your discourse, to the discourse of her through you, are making up their minds, a, their, final decision, passing a judgment on you, your discourse, and hence her—you are attempting to present the best side of her to them, to them as a judging panel, to a jury.[11] This time, though, there is no prosecutor. But even as there may not be an overt attack on her, on the memory of her, every member of the jury is familiar with some aspect of her life that escapes the eulogy, that turns away from any possibility of eulogising; the discourse itself is haunted by its omissions, and these memories that have been marginalised are constantly prosecuting it. So, even as you attempt to quash them—as you play at defending her—you are always also her persecutor.]

---

[11] The possibility of reading a eulogy as a defence in a court of law was opened to me through a conversation on September 7, 2010, with Philadel Yeo, in Singapore.

If we consider the notion that *in the beginning was one's name* and that at the very end all that remains is the name, we then enter the realm where the name has two separate relationalities with time: on the one hand, the name shifts with time, is changed by time, is affected by time (this is the name that lives with the person); on the other hand, a name is always already outside time, at least the time of the person—a name is immortal. But even as one name is immortal, lives beyond the life of the person, this does not mean that it is free from the other changing, constantly shifting, name; the name that dies with the person remains to haunt the immortal name. Perhaps we might even posit that at any one time, everyone has two names—and that one's spectral name is whispering to the other. The problem, the impossibility, lies in determining which one is speaking at any one time.

In invoking the name of the other, we can also never tell which name we are uttering, speaking, speaking with, for, or to—and hence, we can also never quite tell which name we are responding to, with.

But even as we foreground the illegitimacy of authority, of authorship, we should never forget that authority is granted by the other—for, if force, violence, has to be used, utilized, one no longer has authority. In other words, authority is given to us. In the realm of the eulogy, one is usually asked to write, speak, deliver, that particular requiem—this opens the register that one is responding to the name of the dead, even though the request for this response comes from the living (either by way of the family, or when (s)he was alive). Hence, there is a gap between the call for the response and the response itself. Moreover, one cannot deny the fact that one is only an author—writing can only be known—at the moment that one is read: writing, authorship, only comes into being in the reading, through the reader, the other, even if the other is one's self. Thus, not only is the response to the call made in blindness (to where it came from), the response itself is blind to itself until the moment it is called forth (through its reading).

As we are attempting to write, all we can do is to write—after which, all we can do is take responsibility for the particular response by signing off on it.

*stories ... names*

Here, perhaps we should pay attention to the "off" that comes behind, after, with, each signing—for, the only time we actually need to leave our signature on something is if we are going to be away, absent, from it. Otherwise, there would not be a need for us to verify our agreement—our presence—with the sign, a signage, our signing. And this opens the possibility that we have to sign off on our eulogy in case we are not there to read it, speak it—it is not all that uncommon to have someone else read it in our place. But perhaps more than that, each eulogy is in preparation for the eventuality of our own absence.

Each writing, each inscription, is in some way in preparation for our absence: in future-memory of the eulogy that will be written for us—a call for that eulogy that is always already to come.

[This opens the register that every time we write, we are penning our own suicide note; as every writing is what will potentially remain of us when they find us dead. It is our trace—it is an echo of us—even if what is read, the sound that remains, has very little, nothing, to do with us. And it is this that Satoshi Kon captures beautifully in his farewell note to us: anything we write, everything we write, is haunted with Kon's last line—"Now excuse me, I have to go."]

In this manner, all writing is also a eulogy—except in this case a eulogy that doesn't quite know what it is eulogising, or whether it is even eulogising. More than that, the very object of the eulogy remains unknown: for, even as you may be writing for yourself, this very self that you are attempting—perhaps without even any intention—to eulogise continually evades, slips. Here, we might even consider the notion of the eulogy as a call, keeping in mind that whenever you are making a call, you don't quite know not only if it will be answered, nor who will answer it, you don't actually know who you are calling, calling out to, making that call to, until it is answered. All you can do is dial, hold on—wait. And as Vladimir and Estragon have taught us, not only is there no time frame, nor *telos*, to waiting, there is also no object to waiting—even as they wait for Godot, there is no referentiality to the name. Hence, they will not know even if he showed up (he might have always already been there); more than that, even if someone turned up and proclaimed that he is Godot, they would have to take it on faith. Thus, even if Godot came, they might still be eternally waiting for Godot. All they can ever know, all we can ever know, is that they are waiting for Godot, and Godot is the name of waiting itself.

Whenever you write, you sign off. What is left of you is your name. And the marking, your marking, your name, is the very name of your waiting.

[Here, we might momentarily divert and consider the case of anonymous notes, secret letters, and even secret names. Whenever we are confronted with one, there seems to almost always be the natural urge to discover who they came from, the source as it were of their authorship, even to the extent of random attribution (rather than leaving it unknown); as if the lack of a claimant, a signature, opens up the uncomfortable notion that this is a eulogy that could be by anybody, everybody, including yourself—just that you didn't even realise it. Or even worse, that it could be written for you in your absence, in your own death that escaped you.]

In our inability to discern the call, nor the object, of the eulogy, all that we are left with are the tales that are spun—all that we know, insofar as knowing is an attempt to grasp, seize onto, are the effects that the tales have on us. In writing the eulogy, all that can be done is to spin these tales, keeping in mind that as we are weaving them, they are also weaving around, eluding, perhaps even avoiding us. And in the tales that we tell—since the eulogy is haunted by fictionality—all we can tell are stories. Even if, particularly if, we foreground the notion that it is impossible to capture the life of the person. However, in the inability to see, we might be able to catch a glimpse—to echo Michel Deguy when he speaks of poetry—not of the very visible, nor of the invisible, but of the slightly visible.[12]

The name of the story. The story of a name.

---

[12] When I asked Deguy what he thought poetry was, his reply was: "Poetry does not unveil the very visible nor the invisible. Poetry instead unveils the slightly visible." (Saas Fee, Switzerland, August 2004).

*stories ... names*

Where all we can do is tell the tale of a name, her name, spinning around with it, in it, spinning it into the stories that come with it, are built around it, within it; as though all we can do when attempting to eulogise a name is to develop a discourse around it—as if we are sitting for, speaking at, our *agrégation*, only in this case we are being watched, heard, judged by those who are present; even though *la leçon* (in a way we are delivering a lesson on the life of that particular name, even as we are being taught a lesson, being tested on that very lesson that we are giving) might not even be directed towards, at, those very persons.[13]

---

[13] The potential relation between *la leçon* and eulogies was opened to me in a conversation with Chris Fynsk sometime in April 2010. In our particular conversation, Fynsk was recounting his experience of Jacques Derrida delivering a speech—a lesson—on the pun. And this opened the register of the possibility that the name, a name, is the point—the hinge—around which every eulogy revolves, spins; yet at the same time, it is its exteriority, its puncture, as what is foregrounded is the very unknowability of the name, in particular what the name refers to. As we are attempting to pay homage to the name (giving an account of it, being accountable to it, recounting it), we are always also in an almost laughable state of being unable to do so—perhaps even to the extent of us punting on the name, where everyone is taking bets on whether we are ever able to do what we set out to do, as we are racing against time in our attempt to do so.

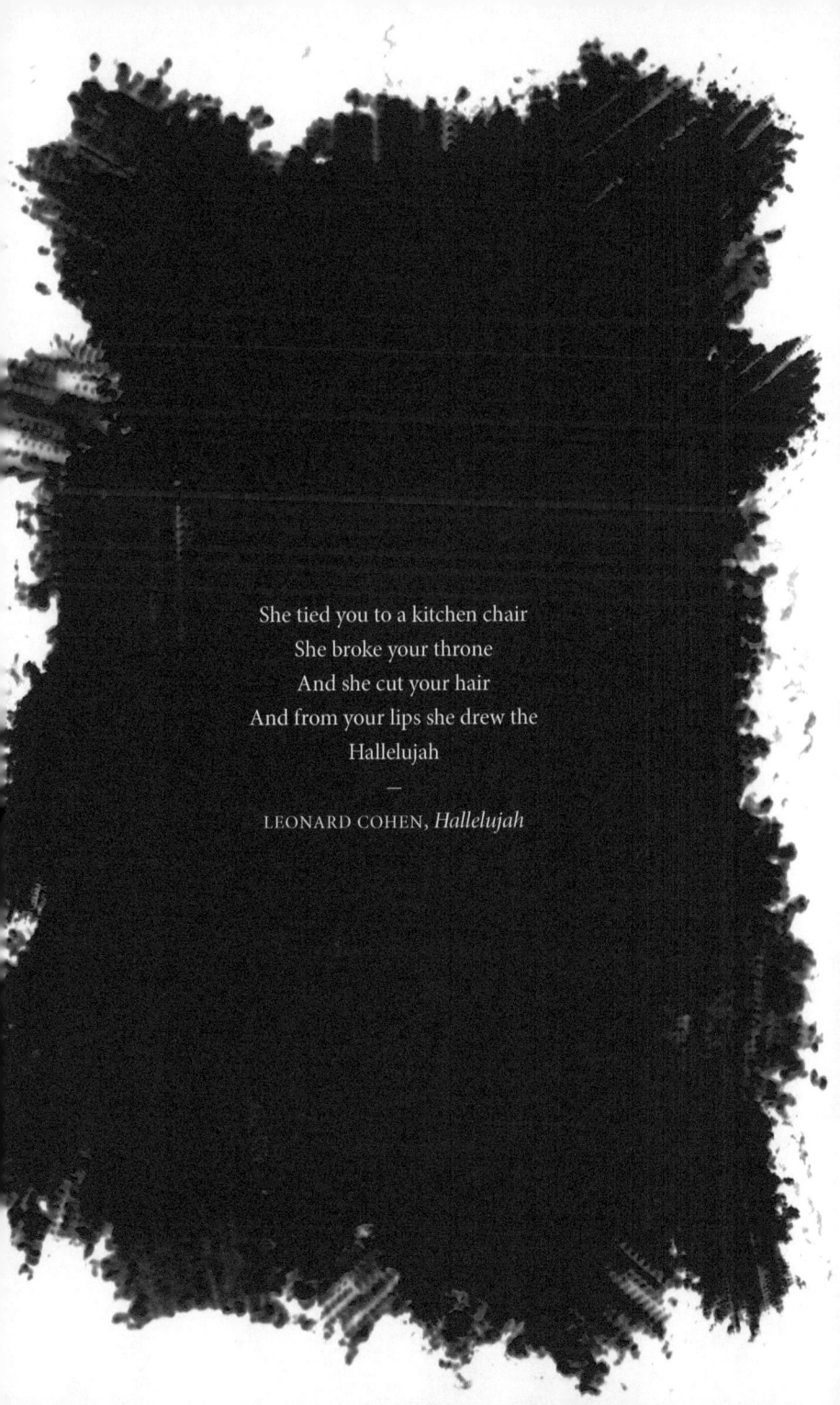

> She tied you to a kitchen chair
> She broke your throne
> And she cut your hair
> And from your lips she drew the
> Hallelujah
> —
>
> LEONARD COHEN, *Hallelujah*

hold,
cut,
kill

> Samson came to my bed
> Told me that my hair was red
> Told me I was beautiful and came into my bed
> Oh I cut his hair myself one night
> A pair of dull scissors in the yellow light
> And he told me that I'd done alright
> And kissed me 'til the mornin' light, the mornin' light
> And he kissed me 'til the mornin' light
> —REGINA SPEKTOR, *Samson*

> *Judas ... must you betray me with a kiss ...*
> —ANDREW LLOYD WEBBER & TIM RICE, *Gethsemane*

Samson and Delilah: a story of betrayal.

"You are my sweetest downfall; I loved you first" (Spektor). Hard to tell from whom these lines came—they could have been from either of them, from both of them. For, even as we are left with that report from *Judges* 13–16, we have to remember that it is a report. From whom, we have no real idea—why they had chosen to report it in that manner is yet another question; one that we might well choose to ignore as we will always remain blind to it. What we have to remember, though, is that we are reading a remainder—Samson is dead; Delilah, we never hear from again.

Delilah and Samson: a tale of forgotten love.

But if it is a remainder that we are reading, are we also always attempting to read a particular forgetting—is it the forgetting itself that is allowing us to read?

Perhaps, then: a eulogy to love.

And if we are contemplating the possibility of a relationality between love and a eulogy, we must then open our receptors to the death(s) in there:

Samson suffers a real death—Delilah's fate is far worse; hers is a symbolic one, relegated to a mere tool of the Philistines, one who is erased the moment the deed is done. Perhaps what we must first pay attention to is the movement from love to death—and here, if we are attentive, we can often hear the cry of betrayal. For, one can only betray someone that one loves, or at the very least, has loved. And even when one is betraying that person, there is still a measure of love in it. When Judas betrays the Nazarene, he is both fulfilling scripture, and also preventing him from mattering "more than the words [he] say[s]" (Webber & Rice: *Heaven On Their Minds*): even as he is giving up the Nazarene to the high priests, there is still an element of fidelity in his action. Even if one were to contend that Judas' intent remains veiled from us, the consequence of his betrayal continues to bear an echo of faithfulness to the fact that the Son of Man had to die. If one were more generous and allowed the possibility of Judas' betrayal being in fidelity to the teachings of the Nazarene, then it is a betrayal of the man in order to protect the ideals he was teaching and stood for, a betrayal of the person out of faithfulness to the idea. But no matter what, in choosing, in picking one over another, there is always already an act of betrayal. And what else is love but a certain selection, a choosing of one out of many others. This is not to say that love is necessarily possessive, claiming, but even if love is an openness to the possibility of another, this potentiality is only opened to some other(s), and not all others. "You are my sweetest downfall"—just you.

To love, one must already betray—cut.

In order to love Delilah, Samson has to first betray Yahweh: he was a Nazirite, and the breaking of this vow caused Yahweh to "turn away from him."[1] Delilah, on the other hand, ostensibly betrays Samson for the love of money, for the "eleven hundred silver shekels" that she is promised in return for discovering "where his great strength comes from, and how we can master him and bind him and reduce him to helplessness."[2] Considering the fact that it is only on the fourth time that Samson gave away the true secret to his

---

[1] *Judges* 16:20.

[2] *Judges* 16:5.

strength, it is no stretch of the imagination to suggest that he had known that he was going to be betrayed—in other words, his love for Delilah was there in spite of the impending, ongoing, betrayal. Here, one could posit that his love for her was so strong as to blind him to her actions: but if we keep in mind the fact that he did thrice offer red herrings, then surely he was well aware of Delilah's plans. In fact, she seems to have made no secret of what she was trying to achieve: each time he told her an alleged source of his strength, she would test it by going "the Philistines are upon you";[3] after which, she would proceed to accuse him of mocking her. More importantly, when he did finally offer her the secret to his strength, he was doing so in full knowledge of the consequences: one could say that allowing her to betray him was his gift of love to her; almost as if he had cut his own hair—all she was doing was providing the shears. In fact, if love were an openness to the other, this would include— cannot exclude—the possibility of being wounded by another; in love, one is always already open to potential betrayal. Perhaps even, one must betray to love, but in loving, one is also always haunted by betrayal.

In considering Delilah's role in their relationality, one is all too tempted to simply cast her as the seductress, a tool of the Philistines to lure Samson's secret from him. Whilst this might have been the overall strategy and result of her efforts, one must not forget that whilst Samson was in prison, "the hair that had been shorn off began to grow again."[4] So, even as "he has told his whole secret to me,"[5] one does wonder if Delilah had passed on all she had known to the Philistines—for, should they have known that "if my head were shorn, then my power would leave me and I should lose my strength and become like any other man"[6] they would surely not have allowed his hair to re-grow; they would not have allowed him to begin to restore his vows, to re-boot his relationship with Yahweh. Perhaps her first betrayal was of Samson; the final betrayal though might have been of her people.

---

[3] *Judges* 16:9, 12, 14.

[4] *Judges* 16:22.

[5] *Judges* 16:18.

[6] *Judges* 16:17.

"But the bible didn't even mention us, not even once …" (Spektor): at least not the tale of love that we are positing, that we are reading, that we are listening to, even as we may not be able to see it. But if we were listening, attempting to respond to a particular call, we may never be able to know if that call was only meant for us, or if it was even meant for us—we may never even know if there was a call in the first place. They, it, may have always been voices in our—my—heads. Perhaps then, it is in reading, in attempting to respond, that we enact our acts of betrayal: in fidelity to one, we have no choice but to choose, to enact a certain death—cut—on the others.

Who ever said that love was two-way? Even if it were mutual, it would consist of two singularities that were in love with one another; an other that remains fully singular, that remains fully other. The other person is an enigma, remains enigmatic. Thus, the reason for that love—why you love the other—is always already secret from the one who loves. This is the only way in which the proclamation "I love you" remains singular, remains a love that is about the person as a singular person—and not merely about the qualities of the person, what the person is. For, if the other person comes under your own schema, then the love for the other person is also completely transparent; one that you can know thoroughly, calculate; the other person becomes nothing more than a check-list. And if it is the qualities that you love, once those qualities go away, so does the love. Only when the love for the other person is an enigmatic one—one that cannot be understood—is that love potentially an event. If so, it cannot be known before it happens; at best, it can be glimpsed as it is happening, or perhaps even only retrospectively. Hence, at the point in which it happens, it is a love that comes from elsewhere: this strange phenomenon is best captured in the colloquial phrase, *I was struck by love* or even more so by *I was blinded by love*. This is a blinding in the very precise sense of, *I have no idea why or when it happened; before I knew it, I was in love.* Cupid is blind for this reason: not just because love is random (and can happen to anyone, at any time), but more importantly because even after it happens, both the reason you are in love, and the person you are in love with, remain veiled from you; you remain blind.

The unknowability in the relationship with the other person suggests that one can only begin to approach it through a ritual. This is the lesson that religions have taught us: since one is never able to phenomenally experience the god(s), one has no choice but to approach them through rites. Being sacraments, they always bring with them an echo of secrets. For, even though one performs a particular ritual, there is no guarantee that one will receive what one is asking for, that the answer might not be something contrary, that there even is an answer. Even as Samson cried out one last time to Yahweh, "Lord Yahweh, I beg you, remember me: give me strength this once again…,"[7] there was no way of knowing if he would be answered.[8] All he knew at that point was that he was about to die—if Yahweh had answered his cry, the pillars would have crumbled and he would have died with the Philistines; if there was no answer, the Philistines would have put him to death for attempting to kill them.

Perhaps that is the secret to love: an offering of death. Not just of all the potential others, but more pertinently of the self.

An offering that knows nothing but the fact that it is offering.

> *Samson went back to bed*
> *Not much hair left on his head*
> *Ate a slice of wonderbread and went right back to bed*
> *Oh, we couldn't bring the columns down*
> *Yeah we couldn't destroy a single one*
> *And history books forgot about us*
> *And the bible didn't mention us, not even once*

Responding to the offering; reading—in that we find the eulogy.

---

[7] Judges 16:28.

[8] Here, we might want to momentarily reopen the register of memory. Since Samson's plea to Yahweh is one that invokes remembering, it opens the question of how he would be recalled by Yahweh. For, his strength would only be returned to him if the recollection was one that reinstated him as a Nazirite; if Yahweh remembered him as the betrayer, he would have continued to turn away from him. Hence, in this plea, in the response to the plea if any, there is a measure of betrayal: Yahweh would have to choose one version of Samson, and cut the other—right before Samson's death, Yahweh had to inscribe his eulogy.

*hold, cut, kill*

The silences we shared
Were testaments of care.
The silence you now leave
A monument of grief.

PETER VAN DE KAMP, *'Testament'*

Stop moping. Cease mourning. And get on with it. Which rather quickly warps into a jeering, a taunting, "go on … get over it." But what are we attempting to cut ourselves off from? For, in order to "get over" a particular "it," there needs to be an object that we can bypass, over-come, go over.

"Pick yourself up"—which usually comes in the form of encouragement, from people that call themselves your friends. The question it brings with it though is—from what fall? And more importantly, why is mourning associated with a falling, a lowering, as if one is no longer fully human, an incomplete person, when one is mourning? What cannot be disputed though is that when we mourn, our lives are sometimes hijacked by that mourning; something does take a hold of you, and at those moments, our mastery of ourselves does go missing. Judith Butler reminds us that in *Mourning and Melancholia*, "Freud reminded us that when we lose someone, we do not always know what it is in that person that has been lost. So when one loses, one is also faced with something enigmatic: something is hiding in the loss, something is lost within the recesses of loss. If mourning involves knowing what one has lost (and melancholia originally meant, to a certain extent, not knowing), then mourning would be maintained by its enigmatic dimension, by the experience of not knowing incited by losing what we cannot fully fathom."[1] In other words, we might not ever know exactly what we are mourning for, let alone why—and in this way, *how* might then always be beyond our grasp. Hence, we are grasped by something that we might never fully grasp, which drives us, compels us, quite often ceases us in its seizing—which suggests that in mourning, even though there might never be an understanding, we are always in a relationality with whomever, whatever, we are mourning. Butler continues: "it is not as if an "I" exists independently over here and then simply loses a "you" over there, especially if the attachment to "you" is part of what composes who "I" am. If I lose you, under those conditions then I not only mourn the loss, but I become inscrutable to myself."[2]

---

[1] Judith Butler. *Precarious Life: The Powers of Mourning and Violence.* (London: Verso), 2006: 21–22.

[2] *Ibid.*: 22.

In trying to "get over it," are we trying to get over ourselves? Or more than that: are we trying to get over the fact that we can never quite get over ourselves?

Amidst all of this, one can also hear the strains of Beckett's "I can't go on, I must go on." Perhaps here, it is also a reminder that one "must go on," when one "can't go on." In this way, the imperative of the "must" is not only an order, but also a plea to go on when one no longer can.

In this all is perhaps a notion of time. As if mourning had a schedule, with an end-point (which can only be known if there is an expected end result, a *telos*, to it). And here, we can hear an echo of one Bush Jr. who announced on September 21, 2001, that the United States was done with—over—grieving, and that it was time for resolute action to take the place of grief.[3] As if one could make a conscious decision to move on—even though one has no idea what exactly one is mourning. In this Bush Jr. is offering a solution, an answer, to a question that has yet to be determined, to a question that is attempting to form itself. And as Avital Ronell has taught us, "the dominant form of stupidity bucks the question entirely; it doesn't allow for questions … ever resisting the question, dominant stupidity on the contrary, effaces it with the quickness of the answer."[4] For, in order to get over it, especially when one has no idea what it is, one has to refuse to think: whether that is actually possible is yet another question. One could posit that there is a denial at play, for there is a certain uncertainty, a certain plunge into the unknown, whenever one mourns. As Judith Butler shows us, "the disorientation of grief—"Who have I become?" or, indeed "What is left of me?" "What is it in the Other that I have lost?"—posits the "I" in the mode of unknowingness."[5] Perhaps then, what we fear most is not just the loss of the other, but ourselves, our own self.

---

[3] 'A Nation Challenged; President Bush's Address on Terrorism before a Joint Meeting of Congress,' *New York Times*, September 21, 2001, p. B:4.

[4] Avital Ronell, *Stupidity*. (Chicago: University of Illinois Press), 2003: 43.

[5] Judith Butler. *Precarious Life*, 2006: 30.

This is not to say that mourning can never end as well—even if there are traces, echoes, in you, which are left in you. However, this is an end that comes to you, perhaps behind your back, and which might not even be known to you, but one that you sense, though maybe only retrospectively. It is a time that comes to you, that calls out to you, and that you have to respond to, just as you had to respond to the call of mourning—where or who this second call comes from is perhaps even less knowable than the first.

But in order to even potentially catch a glimpse of sources, origins, we have to meditate on what it means to respond to a call in the first place.

As one is attempting to respond to a call, one is always haunted by the question of whether one was responding to a call, or is the call always already a reading, an interpretation as it were, a version of the response: in attempting to respond to a call, is one also already writing that call into being. And since this call might have been meant solely for one—even if there are many mourning the same person, there is no way of knowing if it is the same mourning that is taking place—one is in the situation where all one can say is that one is mourning. In other words, one is left with the situation where one can only attempt to respond to the call; whilst never quite being sure if that very call were merely voices in one's head.

It might be helpful to momentarily tune-in to another response, another answer to a call, and consider Werner Hamacher's response to Peter O'Connor and his call, a call for a response. Hamacher asks: "Why is the call thought of as something which, rather than taken, taken down, or taken in— be it from a specific agent, subject, principle, preferably a moral one—will be *given*? And if each call which issues is destined to make demands on the one who is called (but this is also questionable), is it already settled that I will hear, that I will hear this call and hear it as one destined for me? Is it not rather the case that the minimal condition to be able to hear something as something lies in my comprehending it neither as destined for me nor as somehow oriented toward someone else? Because I would not need to hear it in the first place if the source and destination of the call, of the call as call, were already certain and determined. Following the logic of calling up, of the call ... and along with that the logic of demand, of obligation, of law, no call can reach its addressee simply as itself, and each hearing is consummated in the realm of the possibility not so much of hearing as being able to listen up by ceasing to hear. Hearing ceases. It listens to a noise, a sound, a call; and so hearing always ceases hearing, because it could not let itself be determined other than as hearing, to hearing any further. Hearing ceases. Always. Listen ..."[6] As Hamacher teaches us, listening is the openness to the possibility of the other, of the potentiality of being in communication—in communion even—with the other; an objectless other, an other that might be completely other to itself. It is this objectlessness of the other that ensures this communion is one without consumption, without subsumption; the other remains wholly other to ourselves even as we attempt to fleetingly get in touch. Thus, in order to attempt to respond, to be in touch, one has no choice but to momentarily cease hearing, to cut off from hearing the call, whilst at the same time listening, opening one's receptors to everything other than the call. In this way the call remains for one a call, one that might never have been made for one, but a call that one has picked up, and in that manner made one's, even as it is never quite one's; perhaps in attempting to listen—a listening that doesn't purport, pretend, to have an object, objective, aim—all that can be attended to, all that remains, is the very fact that there has been, might have been, a call.

And here, if we listen carefully, we can hear the echo of the telephone. And in particular the call of the phone, ringing; not necessarily for us, but just calling out for a response—as long as we are within earshot of it. Even in this day of caller-identification technology, there is no guarantee that the name flashing on your screen has any correspondence to the person(s) on the other end. The only way in which one can find out who—if anyone—is there, is to pick up. And in doing so, one always already opens oneself to the effects of, to being affected by, another: who hasn't had their day ruined by a bad phone call. This might be true even if there were no known other on the end of the line: for, a prank call often ends up affecting us the most.

---

[6] Werner Hamacher. 'Interventions'. in *Qui Parle: Journal of Literary Studies 1*, no. 2, Spring 1987: 37–42.

In fact, one can posit that one is opening oneself most to the other—almost to the extent of privileging the other—when it comes to calls. As one can never know who is on the other line, each time one picks up the phone, one is opening oneself to the possibility of being pranked, to being made fun of, of facing, coming face to face with, an other that is out to humiliate. Moreover, to even know that it is a joke, a prank call, one has to pick up. And even if one does not speak to the person at the other end, one might already have been affected by the call: no one ever said that we will always like the calls we receive. By picking up one has already paid the price.

And since picking up already entails a response, this means that one will never be able to calculate, verify, know, if one's response to the call is a good one, or not, until after one responds; and even then it is only someone else, another, some other who will decide its status. But regardless of the verdict, the sentence, the judgment of one's sentences, one will always already pay the price for attempting to respond.

Here again, we can hear another crossed line, and pick up on Lucretius' intervention; and in particular, his conception of communication which is a movement away from a transmission, a one-way movement, of information. In *The Nature of Things*, he develops a notion of the movement of atoms, and communication involves the touching, collision, interaction, of atoms from two persons: the negotiations between the atoms take place in a space in-between, film, skin, *simulacra*, and communication is the outcome of the relationality between the atoms. After which, both persons are affected, potentially altered, by this communication, whilst maintaining their singularity. Hence, it would be impossible to claim that there was miscommunication; for, that would have to assume an *a priori* knowledge of what was going to be communicated. If communication happens in the skin, and its effects are only known after the fact, this suggests that all one can say about communication is that it is an attempt to touch the other. And more than that, it is also the opening of the self, an openness, to being affected by another—in ways that one cannot know until it is perhaps too late—to potentially being wounded by the other.

And if we once again pick up another line, open another register of the telephone, we might want to eavesdrop on the pact between Alexander Graham Bell and his brother Melville. In Robert V. Bruce's biography, *Alexander Graham Bell and the Conquest of Solitude*, he notes that both of them made a "solemn compact that whichever of us should die first would endeavor to communication with the other if it were possible to do so."[7] Since Melville was the one who passed on first, this contract put Alexander on the receiving end; in other words, he had to be constantly prepared to receive this call from beyond. In this sense—especially if you were to take into consideration the fact that until Melville's death both brothers had been working on early prototypes of the telephone—the telephone can be read as an attempt for Aleck to maintain the possibility of keeping in touch with Melly. It is this trope, both of hope and of the openness to potentiality, that echoes in the telephone; after all, the instrument of distant sound allows us the possibility of touching the other, even and especially in the absence of that same other. However, this is a connection that is not premised on knowing, but on an openness. And here, we might tap into yet another crossed-line, into *The Telephone Book*, and replay the voice of Avital Ronell that is sitting, housed, in the inbox of our answering machine: "the connection to the other is a reading—not an interpretation, assimilation, or even a hermeneutic understanding, but a reading."[8] This suggests that the very connection between the receiver and the other is the point of connectivity itself; the point of communication is the possibility of this communion.

When one speaks of communion, we can always already hear the echo of "do this in memory of me," an echo that has come to us before, and is perhaps making its second calling. Thus, we might even posit that in communication there is a trans-substantiation that takes place—all persons involved are changed, affected, altered even, but in a manner that might never be perceivable, knowable, known. So, even as one has to cease hearing, even as one has

---

[7] Robert V. Bruce. *Alexander Graham Bell and the Conquest of Solitude*. (New York: Cornell University Press), 1990: 63.

[8] Avital Ronell. *The Telephone Book: Technology, Schizophrenia, Electric Speech*. (Lincoln: University of Nebraska Press), 1989: 380.

to stop hearing the call, one is attempting to do so in fidelity to the call—in order to listen without hearing, to respond without assuming knowledge of the call, to respond without effacing, one has to stop, cut, perform a caesarean, but with love.

This then leads us to the question: if we cease to hear, how can we even begin to respond to a call? For, in order to begin to respond, we must have a notion of who, or what, we are responding to. However, if we already claim to know what, or whom, we are responding to, it is no longer a response in its fullest sense. So clearly, even as we cease to hear, it is not as if we are completely effacing the call; what we are in effect attempting to respond to is a memory—by attempting to listen, we are attending, doing so in memory of the call. All whilst trying not to forget that the memory of the call itself is haunted by the possibility of forgetting.

But perhaps, it is precisely the spectre of forgetting that allows us to even begin to respond in the first place. For, it is our inability to know if we ever know, that leaves a gap in knowing, that maintains the very notion of unknowability in knowing itself, that allows the question to remain in every statement—and what else is this gap but the skin in-between, the simulacra in which, with which, we negotiate with the other; all whilst maintaining the otherness of the other.

After all, one must try not to forget that one cannot be too close—space is needed—to touch.

The inability to know what we are responding to whilst attempting to do so suggests that each response is singular: it happens in a particular time, space, situation, and no matter what the response, what the attempted response is, one can never have the metaphysical comfort, certainty, that the response is correct, or wrong. But just because it is in the realm of opinion does not alleviate our responsibility. If anything, it might actually increase it: after all, if there is no *Grund*, one is choosing a particular path, making a certain decision, based on nothing but the fact that one is. For, each decision always already brings with it a certain measure of violence: in picking, one has no choice but to seize, to separate, to exclude all the other possibilities, all possible others. However, this is an exclusion that is a result of the choosing, a particular decision made in a singular time and space: this is not an *a priori* effacement.

And here, it might be helpful to turn to Jean-François Lyotard and Jean-Loup Thébaud and their conversation in *Just Gaming* when they posit the difference between terror and violence. Terror is a "blow that is not struck on the adversary but it is hoped that the blow will be borne by the third party, the witness, public opinion. In such a case, everyone is caught 'without freedom.'"[9] Violence, on the other hand, is a "two sided battle, [where] my opponent thinks that what I think and do is unjust, and I think that what he does and thinks is unjust. Well his freedom is complete and so is mine."[10] When it comes to terror, one is no longer free to think, one is no longer free to negotiate; one is closed to potentialities. In violence, one maintains an openness to other possibilities, to the possibility of another. In other words, terror is the state where there is no longer any space, where there is no longer any possibility of touching, where there is no longer any other—where there is no longer any communion, only consumption. Hence, terror is the situation where everything is known, everything is clear, calculable.

And it is not as if doing so comes without a price: once something is completely calculable, it is also completely exchangeable, completely transparent. Here, we might momentarily tune in to Jean Baudrillard and attend to his warning that total transparency is the point where "every individual category is subject to contamination, substitution is possible between any sphere and any other: there is total confusion of types."[11] Thus, "each category is general-

---

[9] Jean-François Lyotard and Jean-Loup Thébaud. *Just Gaming.* trans. Wlad Godzich. (Minnesota: University of Minnesota Press), 1985: 70.

[10] *Ibid.*

[11] Jean Baudrillard. *The Transparency of Evil: Essays on Extreme Phenomena.* trans. James Benedict. (London: Verso), 1999: 8.

ised to the greatest possible extent, so that it eventually loses all specificity and is reabsorbed by all the other categories. When everything is political, nothing is political anymore, the word itself is meaningless. When everything is sexual, nothing is sexual anymore, and sex loses its determinants. When everything is aesthetic, nothing is beautiful or ugly anymore, and art itself disappears. This paradoxical state of affairs ... is simultaneously the complete actualisation of an idea, the perfect realisation of the whole tendency of modernity, and the negation of the idea and that tendency, their annihilation by virtue of their very success, by virtue of their extension beyond their own bounds ...."[12] In order for any response to be possible, there have to be boundaries, borders, limits. For, without the separation, the space, one would not be able to even begin communicating with another; everything would just be the same. In other words, what has to be maintained is an exteriority, a finitude to all gestures of knowing. This also means that all responding, all response, is always already finite.

If this were so, a question remains with us: what of the situation in which the call was made? The trouble is: if one can never be sure what the call even is, when, or even where, it came from—if one is blind to both the source and the object of the call—one is attempting to respond to a complete unknown, an absolute unknowability. However, even though there is no possibility of verification, one is still responding—this suggests that there is still a measure of exchange that is taking place. Whether this exchange can be measured is yet another question; one that perhaps can never be addressed. And since there is an exchange that takes place in spite of the fact that the exchange may be impossible, this suggests that the exchange is a symbolic exchange—ritualistic, formal, nothing more—and nothing less—than a form; where the form of the exchange is everything—and in which each individual component is meaningless except for its role within the ritual itself.

And it is this that Georges Bataille speaks of when he describes a *general economy*: everything has its role in relation with every other thing, but

---

[12] *Ibid.*: 9–10.

it has no inherent meaning. Thus, it is the significance of the object and not its signification that is of interest. This is why in Bataille's conception, *sacrifice* plays such a crucial role, where the "essence is to consume *profitlessly*":[13] this is where each exchange is beyond rationality, beyond calculability, beyond reason itself; "unsubordinated to the 'real' order and occupied only with the present."[14] Bataille continues: "sacrifice destroys that which it consecrates. It does not have to destroy as fire does; only the tie that connected the offering to the world of profitable activity is severed, but this separation has the sense of a definitive consumption; the consecrated offering cannot be restored to the *real* order."[15] Since there is no need for a physical change in the object of sacrifice—"it does not have to destroy as fire does"—this suggests that the tie that is severed is ruptured symbolically. And here, we can re-open the earlier register of trans-substantiation when we consider sacrifice: the form remains the same; in fact there is no perceivable change—this is the point at which all phenomenology fails—but there is always already a difference, an absolute separation from the "real order," from logic, calculability, reason. The object of sacrifice, "the victim[,] is a surplus taken from the mass of *useful* wealth … Once chosen, he is the *accursed share*, destined for violent consumption. But the curse tears him away from the order of things …"[16]

And it is this tearing away from the order of things—the order of rationality—that "restores to the sacred world that which servile use has degraded, rendered profane."[17] For, only when it is no longer useful, when it is no longer abstracted—subjected, subsumed under—merely a use-value, can the object be an object as such, can a subject be a subject as such; a singularity. It is perhaps ironic that only within a *general economy* is singularity preserved. However, one must remember that the object—or subject—of the sacrifice is never calculated; its worth is never in question, nor even taken into account. In fact, it is never so much who or what is sacrificed, but the fact that there is

---

[13] Georges Bataille. *The Accursed Share Vol. 1*. trans. Robert Hurley. (New York: Zone Books), 1991: 58.
[14] *Ibid.*
[15] *Ibid.*
[16] *Ibid.*: 59.
[17] *Ibid.*: 55.

a sacrifice. We find in *The Accursed Share* many tales of sacrifice and in each of them there is a sense of reversibility. For instance, in Aztec wars, all deaths were seen as a sacrifice to the gods: if victorious, the Aztecs would sacrifice the prisoners; however, "if the warrior had himself been overcome instead of returning a victor, his death on the field of battle would have had the same meaning as the ritual sacrifice of his prisoner: it would have satisfied the hungry gods."[18] It is this reversibility that can also be found in the tale of Abraham and Isaac.[19] When Abraham brings Isaac up to Mount Moriah as a sacrifice to the Lord, he is asked by Isaac, "… where is the lamb for the sacrifice?" His answer is, "God himself will provide one." Unknown to Abraham at the time, his response (if one can call it a response at all for it was an empty statement; it was neither a truth nor a lie to Isaac),[20] is precisely what occurs: it is God who provides the object for the holocaust—the ram that is burnt in Isaac's place. At the point, in the moment, he raises his knife to sacrifice Isaac, Abraham has already killed him—this is the sacrifice that God required: it is an objectless sacrifice; the act of killing Isaac is the sacrifice; this is the kind of sacrifice that "does not have to destroy as fire does." It does not matter whether Isaac, or the ram, dies: in either case it "would have satisfied the hungry gods." The sacrifice itself is a ritual, is purely formal; the exact object—whether it is a warrior or the prisoner—is irrelevant.

Even though there is no necessary object in the sacrifice, we must never

---

[18] *Ibid.*: 54.

[19] *Genesis* 22:1–19.

[20] One can posit that at this point, Abraham demonstrates a true understanding of communication: it is not so much what is said—in fact the signification of what is said is sometimes completely irrelevant—but that it is said. For, it would have been completely cruel of him to have told Isaac the truth ("you are the ram"). Nor would it have sufficed for him to have remained silent. By answering Isaac with a performative statement, by performing a response to his son's question, Abraham told neither the truth nor lied: all he did was utter a response.

One could constitute Abraham's response as one that resonates with an ironic distance: a response in sound, in form; a response that is responding to the Isaac precisely by not responding. This may well be Abraham being attentive to the very sound of Isaac himself, to the laughter echoing within the one who laughs (*yishhak*: he who laughs)—a moment when the response differentiated the essence from the essential. And what else is laughter but the very rupture of all things, the short-circuiting of everything: where all is heard is a sound; meaningless, but overflowing at the same time.

forget that reciprocity is an obligation. For, even beyond the notions of mores and social obligation, one is always already responding to a call—even the act of ignoring, of not picking up, of making the other redial, call out again, is a response in itself. The only choice one has—the choice that one is obliged to make—is the manner in which one responds. Hence, the difference between terror and violence is that of responses, ways of attending to calls. But just because one has to respond does not mean that there is any knowledge of the response before responding: since it is singular, all that can be known is that one is attempting to respond, and the response is an openness to responding to the call.

And what else is the sacrifice but that of time itself. Time that is sacrificed in responding, to respond, and in response—without which one cannot even begin to attend to any possibility of response. But it is not as if time can be known, or measured; at best, it can be taken into account, accounted for, calculated, after the event, after the response has been made. And even after the sacrifice of time, there is still no guarantee that there is any necessary outcome to the response—in fact, one can never even verify if there was any response to begin with.

Listen. For, that is all we can do. Not because we listen for—there is no necessary object to the call, to a calling. But because there is no call unless we listen; and call the name of the other as we listen.

And even as we utter the name of the other in our attempt to respond to another, to mourn the other, we might want to keep in mind Judith Butler's forewarning that in responding, "I might try to tell a story here about what I am feeling, but it would have to be a story in which the very "I" who seeks to tell the story is stopped in the midst of the telling; the very "I" is called into question by its relation to the Other, a relation that does not precisely reduce me to speechlessness, but does nevertheless clutter my speech with signs of its undoing. I tell a story about the relations I choose, only to expose, somewhere along the way, the way I am gripped and undone by these very relations. My narrative falters, as it must."[21] In attempting to respond, we always run the

---

[21] Judith Butler. *Precarious Life*, 2006: 23.

risk that the very response itself might never get off the runway, might remain firmly stuck to the tarmac, even as we are racing along trying to reach another at the other end of the line. [And in this particular response, in echoing notions of the ground, there is already a response, an "undoing" of the "I" as it is "called into question by its relation to the Other," to another. For, the term "tarmac" came to me through a call, through another, from a distant sound—her, Me-k's, voice—and in resounding it, and fore-grounding its resounding in this retelling, the "narrative falters, as it must." And in that stumbling, we might perhaps catch a glimpse, hear an echo, of that call—in tripping up, perhaps we might actually listen as we momentarily cease to hear.

"To not do by doing"—as she might say.

*get over it*

on
tears

> We must, but we must not like it—mourning, that is, mourning itself if such a thing exists: not to like it or love through one's own tear but only through the other, and every tear is from the other, the friend, the living, as long as we ourselves are living, reminding us, in holding life, to hold on to it.
> —JACQUES DERRIDA, *The Work of Mourning*

What does it mean to cry for another, to tear for them? Barring a performative moment,[1] it is not as if one could will oneself to tear(s)—one is moved to tears, one is taken over, seized, in that moment. Often, one is also ground to a halt, ceased in that moment—and one is nothing other than the very tears that are pouring out of one self. Perhaps it is in that dual movement, the stasis of being grounded, and the frenzy of the outpouring, that we can catch a glimpse of the constant duel that is in tearing itself: as we are crying, there is always already a tearing apart that is going on; a ripping that is not external, nor from a source other to ourselves, but one that is occurring within. For, in some way, we have always known that this moment of tearing happens to us in us, is brought upon ourselves by no one but our self. After all, we can only truly tear for someone that we care for, that we have opened ourselves to, that we have responded to, and called our friend. As Jacques Derrida has taught us, "to have a friend, to look at him, to follow him with your eyes, to admire him in friendship, is to know in a more intense way, already injured, always insistent, and more and more unforgettable, that one of the two of you will inevitably see the other die."[2] To respond to the call of friendship, to respond to the other by calling her your friend, is to already open yourself to the possibility of her death, to the call of death herself.

As we mourn for her, are we also tearing ourselves from ourselves;

---

[1] Even if it is a performance, when one is shedding tears in order to elicit an effect, one is often—especially if the performance is a worthy one—caught in the moment. We see this most clearly in the work of actors, and professional mourners. At the point in which they are crying, they are also seized by those tears, which ends up taking over the performance, and quite often themselves—in that moment, it is often impossible to distinguish the dancer from the dance, the tears from the one who is crying.

[2] Jacques Derrida. *The Work of Mourning*. edited by Pascale-Anne Brault & Michael Naas, (Chicago: University of Chicago Press), 2001: 107.

foregrounding the separation of our self? Is the mourning of a physical death, her death, the closest we can ever come to knowing our own death? For, when our own death comes to us, tears us from our self, it will be a moment that is beyond knowledge, on the outside of knowing—at least any cognitive knowledge that we can speak of now. At best, we can address, think of, death through an imaginative gesture, moment. To even contemplate our own deaths, we need to tear ourselves from our self; we need to imagine ourselves as other to our self. And since there is a gap between the imagined other and our self—otherwise the two would merely be the same thing—even though this space can never be verified—it has to be taken on faith—this suggests that this other within the self is one that is, and remains, wholly other. And if the other remains wholly alterior, mourning is then always already haunted by fiction, and only possible due to fiction itself. In attempting to mourn, we have to read; whilst mourning we have no choice but to write.

Here, we might hear an echo of Thoth, the scribe, the Egyptian god of writing; and in particular Plato's warning from *Phaedrus*: instead of writing being a "potion for memory and wisdom," it would "introduce forgetfulness into the soul of those who learn it: they will not practice using their memory because they will put their trust in writing, which is external and depends on signs that belong to others, instead of trying to remember from the inside, completely on their own."[3] Plato's warning, though, might hint at a form of hope for mourning itself. For, one can never remember an other that is wholly other as such: all one can hope for is to catch a glimpse of that other, an image of that other, and have that other brought to mind. In other words—and here we again have no choice but to speak in the words of the other—this is a figurative re-membering, a reminder, remainder even, of the name of the other; and perhaps by naming the other, even if it is the other within, by using something "which is external and depends on signs that belong to others," we might catch a momentary sight of something. [And this is a something that cannot be named, until perhaps after, but even then it might always remain only a possibility.]

---

[3] Plato. *Phaedrus*. trans. Alexander Nehamas & Paul Woodruff. (Indiana: Hackett Publishing Co.), 1995: 79 [275a].

Perhaps it is this inherent frustration—of naming yet being unable to know what it is one is naming—that can be heard in writing. And here, we turn, tune in, to hear another teaching, that of Avital Ronell, who brings to our attention Martin Heidegger's teaching: "sometimes you have to scream to be heard. This is what Heidegger says regarding Nietzsche in *What is Called Thinking?* Nietzsche, the shiest and most quiet of men had to scream, instituting the most famous inscribing/cry—the *schreiben/schrei, crit/écrit,* or *grito/escrito*—with which philosophy must evermore contend."[4] The fact that we are hearing Ronell echoing Heidegger echoing Nietzsche should not be lost on us here; and this is especially significant if we tune in again to Martin Heidegger when he teaches us that "teaching is even more difficult than learning … because what teaching calls for is this: to let learn. The real teacher, in fact, lets nothing else be learned than—learning. The teacher is far ahead of his apprentices in this alone, that he has still far more to learn than they—he has to learn to let them learn … The teacher is far less assured of his ground than those who learn are of theirs."[5] The question that is opened, then, is one that we hear rather often, almost too often such that it loses some of its significance, that of *so what is all this yelling about?* If there is a certain measure of screaming, crying out, in writing, there is presumably something that is being projected out to, into, the world; something that is being wrenched out of one forcefully, and perhaps even is being thrust onto some other, someone else, who never quite intended to hear it in the first place. Quite often we hear a scream without even knowing where, or whom, it comes from—it can be a noise from afar; which reopens for us the notion of distant sounds, disembodied voices, tele-phones. And in a way the echoing of teachings is a movement of thought, of voice—whether the thoughts are echoed the same way or not is an entirely different question. This is the lesson of the childhood game *Chinese Whispers*: the echo never quite echoes in the same way. Otherwise, there would have been no way for Echo to convey her own echo to Narcissus. In this sense, whenever we are writing, inscribing, a eulogy, even though—and perhaps precisely due

---

[4] Avital Ronell. 'Deviant Payback: The Aims of Valerie Solanas'. in Valerie Solanas. *SCUM Manifesto*. (London: Verso), 2004: 3.

[5] Martin Heidegger. *What is Called Thinking?* trans. J. Glenn Gray. (New York: Perennial), 2004: 15.

to the fact that—we cannot truly know what, or whom, we are eulogising, we are screaming out; and what we are yelling, throwing out, wrenching out of ourselves, is the fact that we are attempting to eulogise whilst being unable to do so. What we are doing is tearing ourselves through our tears, through tearing for.

However, as Heidegger points out, re-echoing Nietzsche once again, "on the one hand, the common idea and views must be shouted at when they want to set themselves up as the judges of thought, so that men will wake up. On the other hand, thinking can never tell its thoughts by shouting."[6] For, "'it is the stillest words that bring on the storm. Thoughts that come on doves' feet guide the world.' (Thus *Spoke Zarathustra,* Part II, 'The Stillest Hour')."[7] Perhaps then, what is most pertinent about writing, the imaginative gesture, the eulogy, is what remains silent—what remains unheard, unhearable even, in, within, all the sound.

In tearing, one always runs the risk of a complete ripping, wounding, where the opening completely ruptures. But each time there is an opening, it is always also a particular closing, a stopping, a cut—caesurae. As it cuts, splits, what remains is the fact that it is splitting from something: the caesurae is never quite complete; a relationality remains. Whether we can know what is held together in that relationality, or how it is joined, or even what this joining is, might always remain veiled from us: however, the fact that in the cutting remains a trace, an echo, of this relationality should not be dismissed. Here, one should try not to forget that a dash separates, but at the same time keeps the separated joined. Perhaps in any separation and joining, in any joining with separation, there is a dashing that occurs, as both bodies propel towards each other, from a distance, no matter how infinitesimal. For, we might also remember that it is a separation—space—that is required for any touching to occur. In this sense, it is the opening, potential wounding, which is necessary for the possibility of touching to occur. Perhaps then it is the screaming, rip-

---

[6] *Ibid.*: 73.

[7] *Ibid.*: 72.

ping, tearing, through writing that is needed for any possibility of mourning, crying, tears.

Which leaves us with the question: if what we are writing, saying, remains unwriteable, unsayable, then what is it that we are saying, writing, as we are not-saying, not-writing? In eulogising, in writing about her, in speaking for the memory of her, what we do—all we can do—is name her. And here, we call upon Martin Heidegger's echo one more time (naming him as we do so): "naming is a kind of calling, in the original sense of demanding and commending. It is not that the call has its being in the name; rather every name is a kind of call."[8] For, as we name him, we have called him to our presence, a summoning that disregards his will—whether he wants to be called or not is irrelevant—we have issued a directive for him to appear before us, not necessarily in person but in thought. Now whether it is his thought or not that appears before us is yet another question—we have dragged this particular notion, line, sentence, statement, from its context; hence, it is a certain reading of Heidegger, with its accompanying violence on him, his work, his *corpus*, we call forth, as we write about it. In other words, the only thing that we truly summon, which is completely separate from us, independent of our thought, wholly other from us, is his name itself. Not just "every name is a kind of call," but more so, *every name is a call, as all we can call is a name.*

So, as we write-speak of her, as we attempt to eulogise in order to mourn, all we are doing is naming her, over and over again, throughout the course of writing-speaking. As we are speaking of her, we are calling her, calling her name to us, to mind; doing this in memory of her.

Her name: naming her, and all others that have her name, at the same time. Her name: offered to her memory—whilst never sure what memory we are offering, or even if the name that we are uttering is her name any longer, was ever even her name. For, (s)he did not give that name to herself: it was her name only because (s)he was named as such. Perhaps her name remains

---

[8] *Ibid.*: 123.

*on tears*

secret, only known to herself. All we can say, all we can utter, is the name that is known to us; and hopefully in that naming, uttering, repetition of her name, we might hear an echo of her name.

All we can do is echo her name, over and over again—in an offering to time.

And in all of this repetition, perhaps, all we are saying—all we can say—is *adieu*.

A book is finished only
when its object has vanished

JEAN BAUDRILLARD, 'Radical Thought'

adieu

The beauty of writing lies—perhaps writing only lies—in the always un-written, the un-writeable; the always imagined, yet outside the realm of the imaginable. This is both the strength of writing and forever its weakness—trying to capture but always failing in representation. The scribbles on a page, the blobs of ink that appear, speak—the phantom of the voice seems to constantly resurrect—of something; an event, an occurrence. But the event it speaks of is always already dead; the word speaks not of it, but of a trans-substantiated event, the ghost of the event—there is necromancy at play.

—

Not that it matters. For the risen event, perhaps akin to a phoenix—a re-generation, a re-incarnation—then takes flight. And develops a life of its own; it is now its own pure image: without reflexivity, without referent, *sans papiers*. And ultimately *sans sens*; for meaning requires an external correspondence. A simulated event is purely internal—it refers to nothing but itself; it speaks of nothing but itself. In this sense, every sign is a meaningless gesture: the *meaning* that is derived is precisely because it is imbued with meaning by its receiver; impregnated by its emptiness. The sign is a vacuum; that is, by its very existence, full. Orphaned at the moment of its birth, it is then embodied by the receiver and already re-born complete with plastic surgery. And it is precisely this sign—which has nothing to do with the event—that draws us into action, an almost arbitrary action: in fact, whenever we act, we are acting on absolutely nothing.

—

In other words, we are always already acting as if we can.

The problem is when we forget this *as if*, and act as though we know what we are doing, as though our actions are based on knowledge, as though everything is clear to us.

—

For, as we were warned, there are consequences to this simulated clarity. This is the point where everything is like everything else, without the ironic distance that *like* and *as if* do not translate to equivalences; similar is not the same—but since everything is taken to be everything else, this is when we move into the point of absolute transparency, and utter meaninglessness.

And not only is meaninglessness the problem. If everything can be flattened, nothing is singular; there is no longer an irreducible difference in humans, in us: we are all completely and utterly exchangeable.

—

What has to be fore-grounded in each act, what we need to remind ourselves to try not to forget, is the potentiality of forgetting.

—

But instead of nihilism, the apex of pure beauty is precisely in this absence. This is where the un-speakable is spoken; through the complete absence of speech. And just like the void that we are inexplicably drawn to—the door that is marked *there is nothing behind here* always already has to be opened—the moment we see it, consideration has already left us. For, it is not as if we can escape signification: we are all born into, thrown into, language. But it is the recognition that all sign systems refer to nothing but themselves that gives us the freedom to play, to imagine, to hope. For, if there is no absolute truth—and perhaps he would even turn that statement on itself—all we are left with is an undecideable, even undecipherable, world. Whilst this may be daunting—there is no longer certainty—this is also liberating; no one can tell you how you should think, or live.

All you have are possibilities.

—

What is at stake is the very possibility of an event.

And it is precisely the singularity of events—an event—that haunts us, that continues to escape all knowing, all attempts to know.

An event, "characterized entirely, in a paradoxical way, by its uncanniness, its troubling strangeness—it is the irruption of something improbable and impossible—and its troubling familiarity: from the outset it seems totally self-explanatory, as though predestined, as though it could not but take place."[1]

Just like death.

One can only utter death metaphorically, naming something that one cannot have a prior experience of; without any possibility of a referent.

Death … a catachrestic metaphor … a pure name.

—

And death is precisely what haunts each name, each act of naming.

Each naming is always already a naming in anticipation of the possibility of death.

—

Perhaps this is why I am refusing to mention his name even as I am speaking about him.

But is it possible to mourn, to say *adieu* without a name: can we ever mourn anything but the passing of a name? For, it is the paradoxical

---

[1] *The Intelligence of Evil or the Lucidity Pact*. trans. Chris Turner. (Oxford: Berg), 2005: 130.

nature of names that allows us to, at least momentarily, approach death. It is only in the foregrounding of the singular-plurality of the name that we escape the banality of clarity, of transparency, of the claim to knowing the person that we are mourning. And which allows us to mourn the passing that was always already in the name, whilst maintaining the absolute alterity of the person; her absolute singularity.

—

And even as we are attempting to bear witness to this passing—for what else are we doing by attempting to speak of something we cannot know about, attempting to speak the impossible—we are faced with the problem of either letting him speak for himself, or attempting to speak for him.

If we are content to speak for him, we risk effacing him, speaking over him, as if he never spoke; silencing him.

If we only allow him to speak for himself, citing him, quoting him, placing those vampire marks around his words (even in full fidelity to him), we are still enacting a violence onto him. This might even be a worse violence to his voice: appropriating it as if it were his words, whilst divorcing ourselves from the responsibility that I am the one that is giving voice to his already silent voice.

Perhaps when faced with this Beckettian paradox, I have no choice but to speak as if I can; I have no choice but to allow him to speak as if he can—I have to vampiricise him, and let him speak through me, as if that were even legitimate to begin with.

And take full responsibility that it is I who am calling forth this voice; as if in a séance, where I am the shaman. Or a telephone.

Here, we must redial on the promise between Aleck and Melly, and recall the promise to listen out for the other, the voice of the other, from the other side.

And pick up the phone.

—

For this moment, though, even as I answer the call, and take full responsibility for answering this particular call over all other calls—just as important, just as relevant—taking into account the fact that this call might never have be meant for me, I shall let the call speak through me, and at most, lend my voice to the call.

But doing so whilst always keeping in mind the static that is in all calls, the silent voices, the ghosts, spectres, hauntings, interjections, interventions; allowing all the different registers to speak, remaining open to the possibilities, forgettings, memories of the to-come, the yet-to-come, the always-already-come. Keeping in mind that all response is elliptical; that when we attempt to respond, we do not hear, but in fact cease hearing, puncture knowing—that all we can do is attend to the possibility of attending;

By listening …

*The absolute rule, that of symbolic exchange,*
*is to return what you received.*
*Never less, but always more.*
*The absolute rule of thought is to return*
*the world as we received it: unintelligible.*
*And if it is possible, to return it a little bit more*
*unintelligible.*
*A little bit more enigmatic.*
—JEAN BAUDRILLARD

Adieu professor …

*adieu*

www.ingramcontent.com/pod-product-compliance
Lightning Source LLC
Chambersburg PA
CBHW021945160426
43195CB00011B/1232